intimate
kisses

ALSO BY WENDY MALTZ

Passionate Hearts:
The Poetry of Sexual Love

Private Thoughts:
Exploring the Power of Women's Sexual Fantasies

The Sexual Healing Journey:
A Guide for Survivors of Sexual Abuse

intimate kisses

THE POETRY OF
SEXUAL PLEASURE

•

edited by
WENDY MALTZ

foreword by THOMAS MOORE

NEW WORLD LIBRARY
NOVATO, CALIFORNIA

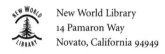

New World Library
14 Pamaron Way
Novato, California 94949

Library of Congress Cataloging-in-Publication Data

Intimate kisses : the poetry of sexual pleasure / compiled and edited by Wendy Maltz : foreword by Thomas Moore.

    p. cm.

Includes bibliographical references.

 ISBN 1-57731-133-7

    1. Erotic poetry. I. Maltz, Wendy.

PN6110.E65 I58 2001

88.81´93538—dc21   00-062208

ISBN 1-57731-133-7
First printing, January 2001
Printed in Canada on recycled paper
Distributed to the trade by Publishers Group West

10 9 8 7 6 5 4 3

CONTENTS

PART 2
self-awareness & discovery   39

PART 3

admiration & appreciation 67

PART 4
union & ecstasy 109

PART 5

afterglow & remembrance **153**

FOREWORD

by thomas moore

I don't believe that anyone knows what sex is. It's the greatest mystery in human life and more profoundly connected with birth and death than we could ever imagine. It's tempting to reduce sex to some pet theory or romanticized idea—the expression of love, communication between lovers, physical ecstasy, a biological need, a spiritual conduit. But I doubt that at a significant level sex is any one of these things.

We do know that sex is close to desire, lust, fantasy, body, love, feeling, union, jealousy, rage, aggression, dream, vitality, failure, transgression, gender, passage. Among the many Greek and Roman deities, each was sexual in a certain way, suggesting that sex itself has many altars and therefore a pantheon of meanings.

If we try to do sex correctly, we fall into a troubling paradox: we get swamped by unwanted desires or we contradict our own values. With sex it's easy to accept the notion that what we repress returns to us. Suppress sexual desire and it comes back to haunt us and to invert our values and expectations. Sex makes many demands, and somehow it seems wisest to respond to them without necessarily taking them at face value. I've counseled many men and women who were at the point of dissolving their marriages because of new sexual attractions. Sometimes it's appropriate to see the poetry in those seductions, and rather than shift to a new partner, to make some changes with the old one or to cope with desire in larger ways.

I think that sex is basically religious, not psychological, and certainly not physical. Nothing human beings do is only physical. Emotions and imagination are always significantly involved. It might even be better to say that sex is primarily an act of imagination, in which, secondarily, the body is included. I realize, of course, that formal religion has enormous battles with sex, because body seems opposed to spirit and desire in conflict with principle. But these battles betray the entropy in religious institutions that have become excessively concerned about rules and moral simplicities. Real religion—affirmation of life, reverence, spirituality, the honoring of mysteries—is profoundly and positively connected to sex. I understand lovemaking as a genuine religious ritual, and I don't mean that metaphorically.

What I appreciate about this collection by Wendy Maltz is that almost every poem takes a particular moment or aspect of sex and turns it inside out to reveal a glimpse of the great mysteries of human experience. In India people are fond of telling the story of Krishna's mother, who looks into his mouth and beholds the entire universe. In a similar way, these poems look at sensuous moments of sex and glimpse the mysteries that make human life so complex and imponderable. These poems go in exactly the opposite direction of social science: they open into the fullness of reality, instead of telescoping it all into moralistic theory and agenda.

Perhaps we can learn from this intelligent and pleasing gathering of poems to see the poetry that sex offers our own lives. Nothing is more important than resisting the literalism and pragmatism we see everywhere around us. Apparently without our knowing it, culture is hard at work trying to kill off the imagination in favor of verifiable fact. Sex is one of the last outposts to resist complete co-opting. It keeps the imagination connected to desire, which is the formula for life. I am grateful beyond expression for Wendy Maltz's achievement. It gives me hope by calling on one of the more significant gifts of sexuality—the sensuous pleasure of well-selected, well-mated words.

INTRODUCTION

*"Sexual love is the most stupendous fact of the
universe, and the most magical mystery
our poor blind senses know."*
—Amy Lowell

Sexual love fascinates me. Like art, music, and dance, it
fills me with appreciation and awe. Sexual love has the
ability to transport us into new realms of experience—
physically, emotionally, and spiritually—realms in which we
come to better understand who we are as sensual, caring
creatures on this earth. And like the arts, sexual love offers
limitless possibilities for human expression and pleasure.

Yet, while we might drop into a conversation how
much we enjoyed visiting an art gallery, dancing the
rumba, or playing the flute, most of us would be rather
reluctant to reveal how deeply we savored an intimate
sexual experience. Sadly, in our culture, we have few
avenues for communicating about the profound beauty

and multitude of pleasures found in the privacy of a loving sexual relationship.

Several years ago I was interviewed on a radio show about my writings on sexual fantasy and the erotic imagination. The interviewer, an athletic-looking man in his forties, seemed very interested when I began discussing an overlooked and under-valued type of fantasy. I call them "sensory" sexual fantasies. Rather than involving a cast of characters or a specific type of sexual activity, sensory fantasies often rely on a single erotic image, such as a flower opening to full bloom, or the sensation of galloping bare-back on a horse. Sensory fantasies can be incredibly arousing. They can amplify sensations, facilitate orgasm, and deeply enhance intimate awareness and connection with a partner.

After the show, the radio announcer confided in me that he experiences these sensory fantasies—a lot. When making love to his wife, he imagines that she is a brilliant diamond and he is a bright ray of sunlight shining through and then shattering outward in all directions from inside her. I was awestruck by his stunning visual imagery, and asked, "Why didn't you share this when we were on the air?" He replied, "You know, it would have been easier to say I picture my wife dressed up as a chambermaid or a dominatrix than to admit I have these kinds of thoughts during sex. I'd never live down the ribbing I'd get from the guys at the gym!"

Unfortunately, our culture inundates us with a steady stream of commercially contrived and artistically limited images of sex. The media boil sex down to turn-ons, impulses, immediate gratification, and power plays.

Popular erotic images and fantasies promote sex that is dissociated from ordinary life, values, personality, feeling, nature, and a healthy relationship. One has only to enter "sexual fantasy" or "sexual love" on an Internet search engine to find literally thousands of provocative pictures of naked strangers engaged in all sorts of impersonal, degrading, compulsive, and abusive sex. Amid this onslaught of depersonalized sex, passionate sexual sharing that is grounded in a caring intimate relationship gets lost.

When sexual love is portrayed in the media, it is often discounted as boring, syrupy, or dangerous. It's rare to see a movie in which two lovers delight in each other sensually, and nothing bad happens to them as a consequence. This is a shame.

Sex within a context of real love, commitment, and safety is expansive and deeply pleasurable. Sexuality surveys confirm this, revealing that people in long-term relationships consistently report having the most frequent sex and the most satisfying sex. We should be shouting this news from the rooftops! At the least, we would be wise to surround ourselves with more inspirations for intimate sex. It's the sublime images of sexual love, such as the radio announcer's diamond-sunlight fantasy, that we should treasure and celebrate.

My goal in creating *Intimate Kisses* is to provide an erotic, yet sensitive, collection of poems that describe sexual pleasure based on intimacy. As a sex therapist and speaker, I have long been committed to offering resources that foster the development of healthy sexual sharing.

My first poetry anthology, *Passionate Hearts,* broke new ground by presenting a rich array of poems that celebrate healthy sex. It describes the development of sexual love in a relationship over time, from courtship to growing old together. *Intimate Kisses* follows up on the success of *Passionate Hearts* by offering more poems that are sensually graphic, sexually explicit, and reflect a positive outlook on love and sex.

Although *Intimate Kisses* is in some ways a sequel to *Passionate Hearts,* this new volume stands alone. The 120 poems in *Intimate Kisses* have their own, unique flavor and focus. Here we journey in a new direction, exploring new depths of erotic experience and intimate satisfaction. From the rich descriptions given by the poets, we discover how erotic imagination can enhance sexual experience and increase sexual pleasure.

I've turned up the heat several notches in this second collection. While still just as heartfelt, the poems in *Intimate Kisses* tend to be a little more sexually direct and explicit. Besides increasing erotic stimulation, these poems can help us discover ways to integrate sexual technique into the kind of heart-connectedness that takes sexual pleasure to new highs in a committed relationship.

I've enjoyed putting this book together. Not only has it exposed me to stimulating ideas and beautiful writing, but it has provided me with an opportunity to explore an intriguing topic: sexual pleasure. Even though I've spent years educating people about sexual anatomy, functioning, techniques, and communication—all important aspects of sexual pleasure—this was the first time I took a serious, in-depth, intellectual look at pleasure.

The idea of sexual pleasure is riddled with shame and confusion. In our culture, we're often encouraged to seek it but shamed for feeling it. A client once told me that the messages she heard growing up taught her: *If it feels good, it must be bad.*

Negative messages about sexual pleasure cause a lot of unnecessary personal suffering. They generate feelings of anxiety, embarrassment, inhibition, fear, and alienation—all of which get in the way of enjoying sex. We can use resources, such as this book, to help us get past these barriers to pleasure. Examples of people who are freely and unequivocally delighting in healthy sexual sharing show us another view of sex, another way of understanding pleasure. And, the more we understand about sexual pleasure, the more we can open to it and cultivate it in our own lives.

As I began accumulating a sizable number of poems

to choose from for this collection, certain characteristics about sexual pleasure became apparent: There are many different types and intensities of sexual pleasure. Some sexual pleasures are far more "pleasurable" than others. What is extremely pleasurable to one person may not be to another. Individual preferences for sexual pleasure can change as we grow and change and encounter new experiences.

I found myself most attracted to poems describing experiences that are pleasurable on many levels. The sexual contact is personally enhancing, sensually enjoyable, mutually delightful, and emotionally intimate all at the same time. These poems illustrate how rewarding sexual interaction is when a conscious connection exists between one's heart, one's genitals, and one's lover. Sex that is enjoyable on many levels catalyzes personal energy and aliveness. It leaves us feeling relaxed in mind and body, as well as content in spirit.

Developing this collection put me in touch with the power of poetry to describe profound human experience. Good poetry involves breath, movement, pulse, rhythm, and flow—qualities also found in pleasurable sexual experience. It's no wonder that many famous lovers are noted for their use of verse in courtship.

No one can better teach us about sexual pleasure than poets. Their well-chosen words take us beyond our limited life experiences and show us the unlimited potential for expression. For example, many poems in this collection describe the interplay of opposing energies, so common in passionate experience. Notice how well an anonymous sixteenth-century poet was able to capture the dynamic shifts of contrasting energies in this lively poem, "The Enjoyment":

> ... *Darting fierce and flaming kisses,*
> *Plunging into boundless blisses,*
> *Our bodies and our souls on fire,*
> *Tossed by a tempest of desire*
> *Till with utmost fury driven*
> *Down, at once, we sunk to heaven.*

Another quality of poetry that makes it an excellent art form for describing the intricacies of sexual pleasure is its reliance on imagination and metaphor. As the late pioneering sex therapist Helen Singer Kaplan would say: "Sex is composed of friction and fantasy." What goes on in our minds is as important as what happens in our bodies. Senses come alive in highly pleasurable sex. We experience heightened consciousness and connection. Emotion, sensation, and thought intertwine in imaginative ways, enhancing experience.

The sensory imagery of poets gives us surprising new visions of beauty. One of my favorite metaphors in the collection is in Walter Benton's poem "Entry June 12" in which he uses unique imagery to honor the beauty of his lover's body:

> ... *Yes, your lips match your teats beautifully, rose and rose.*
> *The hair of your arm's hollow and where your thighs meet*

agree completely, being brown and soft to look at like a nest
        of field mice.

The poems in this collection demonstrate how our senses can merge and become confused in great sex. Poets frequently use a process known as "synesthesia" to blend one sensory element with another. Here is an example from Leatha Kendrick's poem "It":

My eyes whiten, they widen
as if this feeling could be eaten
savored on the tongue of vision,
one gulp seeing feeling.

The title of this collection emerged naturally from the works themselves. The poems describe an entertaining assortment of *intimate kisses.* Some of these I had not considered before, such as cloud kisses, moth kisses, backbone kisses, orange kisses, belly-to-belly kisses, lyrical kisses, coffee-flavored kisses, and suction squeaking kisses. In reading this collection, listen for how many different times and how many different ways kisses occur.

It's no coincidence that there are so many kisses in this collection. Kisses, whether they are with the eyes, the breath, or the toes, allow us to touch and connect emotionally, as well as physically, with a partner. The more intimate the kiss, the more profound the connection.

Organizing and sequencing the poems led me to some other new discoveries. We can view sexual pleasure from different perspectives along a continuum of time.

Some poets describe pleasure in terms of what they want or hope to experience. Others describe the immediacy of an actual sexual encounter. Still others find pleasure in reflecting on past sexual sharing. Seeing sexual pleasure in this new way—from anticipation, through experience, to remembrance—helps us become more aware of the infinite and subtle delights we can tune into any time, not just during sex.

The natural sequencing of the book reinforces something I've learned as a sex therapist. People like different things about sex. Some treasure the foreplay and slow building of excitement. Others enjoy the rush to and release of climax. Others savor the warm closeness of lying in their lover's arms after sex. Thus, the poems can familiarize us with pleasures we haven't yet experienced or imagined.

The book is grouped into five distinct parts, which reflect how sexual pleasure unfolds in the course of an evolving intimate relationship. Often, we begin a relationship focused on what we hope to experience. Next, we tune into how new and different we feel being with the partner. Then, turning from self to other, we appreciate the special qualities of our partner. Next, we delight in how close we can get as a couple. Later, we take pleasure in remembering good times we shared.

The opening section of the anthology, "Anticipation & Desire," contains poems that describe the pleasures of looking forward to sexual closeness. Here the poems speak of sexual attraction, sexual longing, and the promise of fulfillment. Whether it's a new relationship or one that's settled into long-established patterns, there's much to enjoy in the courtship stage of sex. Russell Leong has written, "Eroticism is the fruit born of the delicate tension between the repression and the expression of sexual desire."

It can be exciting just to know that one's lover will soon arrive for a planned rendezvous. Marge Piercy gives us a delightful view of "Little Acts of Love," the small domestic rituals leading up to a sexual encounter:

> ...A new paisley cloth on it,
> I sit at the table
> studying recipes.
>
> Each recipe is a dance
> of seduction, beckoning.
> Soon the door will swing wide
>
> to where I wait in my body
> crowned and glittering
> for the feast to start.

In David Meuel's "What Makes It Good," we get a sense of how exciting it is to receive a sexy flirtation from a partner:

> ...it's
> the spinning waters way I feel
> when you grab me by the eyes
> and slip your thin black panties
> off

Sometimes it's fun to actively engage the partner in a dance of seduction. Nikki Giovanni creates a rocking, playful rhythm in her song-like invitation to sex, "That Day":

> ... *if you've got the dough*
> *then i've got the heat*
> *we can use my oven*
> *til it's warm and sweet*
>
> *i know i'm bold*
> *coming on like this*
> *but the good things in life*
> *are too good to be missed...*

Robin Jacobson's poem "The Dance" reminds us that by slowing the dance of courtship and arousal, we can appreciate new pleasures in each step:

> ... *Our bodies urge us, they say*
> yes, *and* oh yes. *But the waiting*
> *is so sweet we choose it, we linger*
> *at each brush of lip on lip as if it were*
> *new wine, to be rolled around the mouth*
> *before we swallow. Once, anticipation*
> *was something to outrun.*
> *Now it's what we love most...*

In Part II of the collection, "Self-Awareness & Discovery," the poems reveal how profound experiences of sexual love can be in raising our own awareness of who we are, physically, sensually, and emotionally. In the context of an intimate relationship, we can become more in touch with our own power, beauty, and ability to feel and evoke sensation and love.

Listen to the speaker in Anne Sexton's "The Kiss" as, after having received a partner's touch, she discovers herself capable of feeling a full, intense range of sexual sensation:

> *. . . Before today my body was useless.*
> *Now it's tearing at its square corners.*
> *It's tearing old Mary's garments off, knot by knot*
> *and see—Now it's shot full of these electric bolts.*
> *Zing! A resurrection!*

By contrast, in "Touch," Octavio Paz describes the satisfaction that can come from being aware of one's own ability to influence and pleasure a partner:

> *My hands*
> *open the curtains of your being*
> *clothe you in a further nudity*
> *uncover the bodies of your body.*

Opening to sexual love and pleasure often involves overcoming feelings of guilt and inhibition. As couples safely experiment with new sexual positions and activities, it's not uncommon for partners to realize they enjoy something they once considered unacceptable or strange.

Sharon Olds gives us a look into a woman's mind as she views herself on all fours in a mirror while making love, and arrives at a moment of profound self-acceptance of her primitive nature and deep enjoyment of sex. In "I Cannot Forget the Woman in the Mirror," she writes:

> *... she was so clearly an*
> *animal, she was an Iroquois scout creeping*
> *naked and noiseless, and when I looked at her*
> *she looked at me so directly, her eyes so*
> *dark, her stare said to me I*
> *belong here, this is mine, I am living out my*
> *true life on this earth.*

In "Admiration & Appreciation," the third section of the anthology, the poems describe an intimate appreciation for the partner. This enjoyment of the partner goes beyond initial infatuation. It involves a cherishing of the partner's unique physical, sensual, and emotional qualities. With each lovemaking, we build associations of pleasure with every detail of the partner's body. Our partner's body becomes a familiar, yet continually intriguing source of erotic excitement.

Audre Lorde, for example, describes in sensuous detail her lover's breasts as "warm as sunlight," her lips "quick as young birds," and the flavor between her thighs as "the sweet sharp taste of limes." And Edward Kleinschmidt Mayes celebrates the tip of his lover's tongue as it

> *... [traces] the map*
> *of my body, the inroads,*
>
> *rugged terrain, back*
> *alleys, wilderness areas. The tip of your tongue*
>
> *is the tip of the world....*

In this section on the appreciation of partners, a specificity of language designates the person we love as unique and utterly desirable, and shows how our beloved arouses us as no one else can.

In "The Ninth Secret Poem," French poet Guillaume Apollinaire chants a delightful tribute to a partner's beauty and attractiveness. Here are just a few lines:

> *... I am the hauler of your midnight hair*
> *O lovely ship on the canal of my kisses*
> *And the lilies of your arms are beckoning me*
> *O my summer garden*
> *The fruits of your breast are ripening their honey for me*
> *O my sweet-smelling orchard....*

Sometimes in the face of such perfection we fall speechless, for the power of our passion can overwhelm language. Carolyn Flynn expresses this well when she writes:

> *... You want to know what I see*
> *And I stand mute before you*
> *Unable to find metaphor*
> *For a life form so deliciously itself....*

This poem's brilliance lies in its ability to communicate what it's like to fall mute before a lover, while at the same time giving voice to the transcendent beauty of the moment.

New Zealand poet Trudi Paraha reminds us of how, when we deeply care for another person, we can be moved to call our partner by an endearing nickname. In the native language of Paraha's Maori tribe, the title of her poem "Whaia i te Po" literally means "to search in the night." By extension, calling one's lover "e whaiaipo" is a way of saying, "You're the one I search for in the night."

> *... and how i've gone*
> *mad in heart for that*
> *sunlicked look of you*
> *e whaiaipo*
> *let's off to bed and play*
> *i want to paint a love poem*
> *all over the sheets and you*

In Part IV, "Union & Ecstasy," poets write of the experience of mutual discovery and creation. Here we get a sense of how sharing sexual pleasure can strengthen the emotional bond two partners feel for each other.

Listen to descriptions of equality, mutual sharing, and new creation that reverberate from Roger Pfingston's lovely poem "Occasion":

> *... We crawl*
> *through each other*
> *and back again*
> *guided by our blood-*
> *electric finger tips.*
> *I swim in you,*
> *you in me until we*
> *drift down, slowly*

settling in anemone
of pillowed hair,
entangled leg and arm,
beneath our tongues
a dream of fruit,
tide of sunlight
inching over the dark
planetary coast.

Elizabeth Barrett Browning writes of the strangely pleasurable, utter disorientation that can occur when love has connected us so deeply with our partner that we no longer know where we end and they begin.

. . . And, as we sate, we felt the old earth spin,
And all the starry turbulence of worlds
Swing round us in their audient circles, till,
If that same golden moon were overhead
Or if beneath our feet, we did not know.

Many of the poems in Part IV use imagery and metaphors from nature. This is no coincidence. Ecstatic sexual experiences reinforce our connection to nature. We are reminded of our intrinsic link to the universal elements of fire, water, earth, and sky. Lovers "reel with the rip and tide of ocean," "rise and float away on teeming pleasure," and "open and flame with a delight that never stops." Similarly, the joy of sexual union resonates through the different seasons from mornings in "the good old summer time" to nights when the "snowflakes flutter down outside the bedroom window."

While metaphors from nature are not limited to this fourth part of the anthology, here they often seem stronger and more climactic. Perhaps this is because, as author John Welwood writes, sexual communion lifts us out of the narrow shell of personality and "puts us in touch with the larger energies of life flowing through our bodies. Thunder, lightning, electricity, rain, moonlight, and sunshine..."

The final poem in this section is by Galway Kinnell. After describing in lively detail the sexual dance of the couple, he shows them slipping into sleep and notes:

> ... If someone were to discover them this way,
> him like the big, folded wings of her,
> they might stay as they are, the way the woodcock,
> believing herself safe in her camouflage, sometimes
> sits still until a person stoops and reaches out to pet her—
> then jumps six feet straight up and wherries off...

And when the couple wake, Kinnell evokes the collapse of conventional time that lovers experience when they lose themselves in the power of sexual pleasure:

> ... They hear the clangs of a church clock. Why only nine?
> When they have been lying on this bed since before the earth
> began.

As we move into the book's final section, we shift from the present or immediate past into a mode of nostalgia. In Part V, "Afterglow & Remembrance," poets describe their deep appreciation for the experience of sexual connection.

Here lovers linger in the afterglow of intimacy, not yet concerned about the future, only enraptured by the dizzying dance they shared in each other's arms.

In her poem "Afterwards," Dorianne Laux describes the companionable silence and relaxed satisfaction that two lovers share as they emerge from the throes of passion:

> . . . our breath slowing, our heads tipped
> and touching at the crown,
> like a couple of kids
> slumped on a dock in the sun, our legs
> dangling above the bright water,
> admiring each other's reflections.

There is a sense of tender gratitude in this last section, as in "Listener" by Joseph Millar. His poem expresses the quiet wonder at the personal healing and nurturing that can result from emotionally honest love-making.

> . . . What still country have I come to,
> where the long grass bends under the animals
> when they lie down, emptied of suffering?

In a similar vein, Elizabeth Claman's "Love & Desire" uses original imagery to evoke the sense of closeness and celebration felt after sex.

> . . . Joining in as many ways and grateful.
> Even my hair this morning is glad.
> And the sky, who sometimes has her reasons,
> comes down gently all around us,

touching her blue hem to every particular
until the whole cake rises in the sun!

A number of the poems in this last section speak to the power of sexual attraction, surfacing even after lovers have been "long at it." Sexual pleasure initiates desire for more sexual pleasure and closeness, just as a good meal whets your appetite for the next feast. Jonathan Blake's poem "Myth" contemplates this cycle of desire:

... both of them seeking a perfection they know
doesn't exist but insisting like all lovers
again and again on its possibility.
The mystery of the sweetness never revealed.
Only more familiar. Visiting what they believe
to be godly within ...

The poems inform us about another aspect of richly rewarding sex: the ability to last and to be integrated in future experience. Like the satisfaction of later reflecting on a great symphony or a memorable vacation, poets share with us how they were able to take a wonderful sexual experience and carry it with them into their subsequent experiences. I love the line from June Sylvester Saraceno's poem in which she says, "your last kiss lingers long after the ordinary day begins." And Neil Carpathios gives us an amusing glimpse into one man's post-coital reminiscing in a Victoria's Secret lingerie shop. He's spotted by the clerk, "fingering the lacy cups." All the while he thinks of his lover's "pendulous orbs" swinging above his "naked nights" and "boxing his ears."

As the anthology draws to a close, we move again into a deep sense of the way sexual love seems so much larger and more captivating than anything else in life. The poets seem struck by the power and mystery of it all. In "A Moment," Abraham Linik asks the question, "What is it that matters? What is it that lasts?" If there is an answer, perhaps it involves accepting the transitory nature of ecstatic experience.

Time and again the poems teach us that we cannot hold on to the physical experience of sex any more than we can capture the beauty of a sunset or the mating call of a bird in flight. Indeed, the fleetingness of sexual pleasure is what makes it so breathtaking.

Learning from the poets, we can cultivate our awareness of these passing erotic moments. And even if words fall short of capturing the depth of our experience, we will have recognized the sexual intimacy in our own lives as something rare, profound, and worthy of celebrating again and again.

As Audre Lorde reminds us, "The erotic is...an internal sense of satisfaction to which, once we have experienced it, we know we can aspire. For having experienced the fullness of this depth of feeling and recognizing its power, in honor and self-respect we can require no less of ourselves."[1]

[1.] Audre Lorde, from "Uses of the Erotic: The Erotic as Power," in *Sister Outsider* by Audre Lorde. Santa Cruz, Calif.: Crossing Press, 1984.

PART 1

anticipation & desire

"Let us be candles..."

THE REAL HEARTH

Let's heat up the night to a boil.
Let's cook every drop of liquid
out of our flesh till we sizzle,
not a drop of come left.

We are pots on too high a flame.
Our insides char and flake
dark like sinister snow idling down.
We breathe out smoke.

We die out and sleep covers
us in ashes. We lie without
dreaming, empty as clean grates.
Only breath moves hissing.

Yet we wake rebuilt, clattering
and hungry as waterfalls leaping off,
rushing into the day, roaring
our bright intentions.

It is the old riddle in the Yiddish
song, what can burn and not burn up,

a heart, a body, passion that gives
birth to itself every day.

The body does not wear out with
use, nor does love, so let us
use each other in the best of ways
as the hours jump off the cliff.

marge piercy

WILD NIGHTS—WILD NIGHTS!

Wild Nights—Wild Nights!
Were I with thee
Wild Nights should be
Our luxury!

Futile—the Winds—
To a Heart in port—
Done with the Compass—
Done with the Chart!

Rowing in Eden—
Ah, the Sea!
Might I but moor—Tonight—
In Thee!

emily dickinson

LINEAMENTS OF DESIRE

going down from the attic
you hold the ladder
as I descend
the afternoon light

we pause on the porch
to catch the sun as it falls
behind the horizon of houses
and I smile at the flashes
of copper in your beard

in the blinding brightness
you stand between me
and the sun setting
tendrils ablaze

a warm summer breeze
ruffles your hair
and the unbuttoned
loose fitting
striped cotton shirt
that covered your chest
all day in soft folds

as you lift your hand
to lean on the white
stucco wall of the house
the front of your shirt
like the flap of a tent
falls open

a slant ray of sun-
light shadows the hair
on the skin of your arm
and your chest
now bare
draws my glance

my eyes flicker down
to the curve of your breast
and the nipple at the center
of the cheek of your breast

looking away
then glancing again
my eyes alight
where my lips would linger

though I dare not
rest my head on the rise

of your chest
my eyes trace the naked
line of your flesh
to the nipple I would touch
with the tip of my tongue

patti tana

The moth's kiss, first!
Kiss me as if you made believe
You were not sure, this eve,
How my face, your flower, had pursed
Its petals up; so, here and there
You brush it, till I grow aware
Who wants me, and wide ope I burst.

The bee's kiss, now!
Kiss me as if you entered gay
My heart at some noonday,
A bud that dares not disallow
The claim, so all is rendered up,
And passively its shattered cup
Over your head to sleep I bow.

robert browning

—from "In a Gondola"

THE DANCE

On the walkway above the summer creek
we touch and kiss, your hand cups
the long smooth muscle of my back,
we move to the pulse of valve and blood.
Our bodies urge us, they say
yes, and *oh yes.* But the waiting
is so sweet we choose it, we linger
at each brush of lip on lip as if it were
new wine, to be rolled around the mouth
before we swallow. Once, anticipation
was something to outrun.
Now it's what we love most,
the slow, slow build before,
like all the little moments of our lives
gathering toward the last breath.

robin jacobson

LITTLE ACTS OF LOVE

Shaking out clean sheets
that crisp lightly scented caress,
I make my bed ready for you.

I wash my hair, trim
nails lest they scratch you—
unintentionally.

A new paisley cloth on it,
I sit at the table
studying recipes.

Each recipe is a dance
of seduction, beckoning.
Soon the door will swing wide

to where I wait in my body
crowned and glittering
for the feast to start.

marge piercy

THIRST

Like a blade of summer grass
turning towards a fragrance
of rain caught in the air's
cooling, I come back to you.

How the dry thirsting reaches
for even the resemblance
of wetness, its parched brown
skin drawn tight and leaning

into the promise of moistness.
I feel also this pull
stretching me to breaking.
If soon your kisses do

not drop on me—mist,
shower, or flood—I will
split into thin slivers, be
cut down like so much hay.

linda alexander

FIRES

Your ax nicks
chips for tinder,
splits a block in two
strips that please you
with their kindling
power. Next you sink
the blade so deep into
a thicker log it stays
in place as you lift.
I listen to the pock
of wood on brick as you
work the last stakes
of oak free and sit
back on your tawny
haunches, breasts exposed
where your robe has fallen
open, waist-length hair
tucked into a faded Brooklyn
Dodgers cap to save it
from the flames that will
come of this.

In my hand, one long slip
of bark you peeled
for its scent rests
like a second skin.
I could not be
more ready for your
touch, but wait to watch
you light the day's
balled news of chaos
in Kazakhstan and poke
the blaze with a forked
madrone branch. Soon there
is fire between us
again and more heat
than we can bear.
Our shadowy pattern
flickers on the peeling
wall. My body fills
with warmth where it is
touched by the glowing
of your fires.

floyd skloot

BLACK WATER

Black blazing night. My heart
pounding, I hear
your heartbeat under my hand,
we pause beneath the trees
to kiss. Hike on down
from the high woods.
                  Loud
rush of wings. Wind falling
silent in the pines. You and I
follow the old bear trail trampled
clear to the shore: Rocks,
rubble, sedge grass tall
in the shallows. No moon
on the lake. Stars
spark and shine.
                  Alone
through the dark we watch
two ducks tuck in, drift together.
On the pine shore we lie down—
I want to feel your breasts turn
firm in my palm. Your tongue
in my mouth when our legs open.
In the moist fur the fold

encloses me. And when we part
I want to lie with you
the way night lies on deep water—
On the slow breathing lake
two wild ducks float
side by side, asleep
on still water. Black water.

george keithley

WHAT MAKES IT GOOD

isn't
the mystery or masterly technique
or even a love so strong
you can smash bricks with it

it's
the spinning waters way i feel
when you grab me by the eyes
and slip your thin black panties
off

david meuel

SHAVING NIGHT SONNET

I can't help but watch the blade reveal
the face behind the man. Each careful stroke
reshapes the curves my fingers itch to feel.
I'd trace—so soft—your jaw, your lips, your nose
and never nick or scratch your tender skin
if you'd abandon that cold blade for me.
My hands would kiss the spot above your chin;
they'd sculpt the lids below your brow and see
just where your slow, lovely lines would lead.
Again you dip your soap edged sword and stir
the heat to steam; it rises, mists. It beads
and paths of silver fingers stripe the mirror.
Finally, you stop, so smoothly turn and trace
the lips that, line by line, reveal my face.

debra pennington davis

COME WITH ME TO OUR SWEET BED

Come with me to our sweet bed
our sweet white bed
yellow bed   blue quilted bed
oh the long warm limbs
and the soft of our belly
nuzzling lips to shoulders
holding you   holding me
our eyes   open   our eyes
open even when the tears
run out the corners and
mix on our cheeks
our mutual pillow
I would be in you
here are my breasts
take them   here is your
entering me   so deep so
deeply come with me
to our sweet bed

penny harter

THAT DAY

if you've got the key
then i've got the door
let's do what we did
when we did it before

if you've got the time
i've got the way
let's do what we did
when we did it all day

you get the glass
i've got the wine
we'll do what we did
when we did it overtime

if you've got the dough
then i've got the heat
we can use my oven
til it's warm and sweet

i know i'm bold
coming on like this
but the good things in life
are too good to be missed

now time is money
and money is sweet
if you're busy baby
we can do it on our feet

we can do it on the floor
we can do it on the stair
we can do it on the couch
we can do it in the air

we can do it in the grass
and in case we get an itch
i can scratch it with my left hand
cause i'm really quite a witch

if we do it once a month
we can do it in time
if we do it once a week
we can do it in rhyme
if we do it every day
we can do it everyway
we can do it like we did it
when we did it
that day

nikki giovanni

Spring paints the countryside.
Cypress trees grow even more beautiful,
but let's stay inside.

Lock the door.
Come to me naked.
No one's here.

jelaluddin rumi

—translated from the Persian by
　Coleman Barks with A. J. Arberry

SKINSONG

Come when it's quiet
I like your way of moving
Slip into my stillness
Silence me

Speak in tongues
Anoint the air between us
Dance to a skinsong
Cover me

trudi paraha

PEELING AN ORANGE

Between you and a bowl of oranges I lie nude
Reading *The World's Illusion* through my tears.
You reach across me hungry for global fruit,
Your bare arm hard, furry and warm on my belly.
Your fingers pry the skin of a navel orange
Releasing tiny explosions of spicy oil.
You place peeled disks of gold in a bizarre pattern
On my white body. Rearranging, you bend and bite
The disks to release further their eager scent.
I say "Stop, you're tickling," my eyes still on the page.
Aromas of groves arise. Through green leaves
Glow the lofty snows. Through red lips
Your white teeth close on a translucent segment.
Your face over my face eclipses *The World's Illusion.*
Pulp and juice pass into my mouth from your mouth.
We laugh against each other's lips. I hold my book
Behind your head, still reading, still weeping a little.
You say "Read on, I'm just an illusion," rolling
Over upon me soothingly, gently moving,
Smiling greenly through long lashes. And soon
I say "Don't stop. Don't disillusion me."

Snows melt. The mountain silvers into many a stream.
The oranges are golden worlds in a dark dream.

virginia hamilton adair

I WANT TO SING

i want to sing
a piercing note
lazily throwing my legs
across the moon
my voice carrying all the way
over to your pillow
i want you

i need i swear to loll
about the sun
and have it smelt me
the ionosphere carrying
my ashes all
the way over
to your pillow
i want you

nikki giovanni

I WOKE UP

kissing your neck.
Was it the storm outside or
the storm in my dream made me open
my eyes? I lowered my eyes
when you looked at me knowing
I came to your bed desiring
this joining. Your look is kind but
cautious. Releasing a breath, petals
unfolding the fist of a flower,
I rest my head on your shoulder
as always, and now I am kissing
your neck. This time I'll not stop
with the skin of your beard,
this time I will moisten
everywhere lips and tongue
can touch beyond words,
always the words did the touching but
now I will swallow your words
tender words the breath in the ear
will speak for us now
we are so close there's laughter
where my lips are touching

and lifting my eyes to see your lips
spread in a smile
I wake up kissing your neck

patti tana

BREAKFAST IN BED

The smell of yeast and sweat
    Surrounds the mound
Of soft and tender dough.
    I flour my hands
And knead the folds and flaps.
    They look powdered.

They make me think of you,
    My hands on your
Spread thighs, your hands in my hair,
    My tongue at work,
Your rising milky heat.

    The mound grows smooth
And firm, a sweaty gloss
    On its tan skin,
And I recall your breasts
    When your nipple
Is in my mouth and my hands
    Grasp their plump sides.

Everything begins
    To rise. Soon I'll
Climb the stairs to wake you
    For our breakfast
In bed, long hard fresh-baked
    Loaves and our juice,
A sticky, hot repast
    Between our legs.

michael s. smith

A SIMPLE PLEASURE

The better part of morning is
to lie waking knowing she is near
and coming back
her face washed alive, her hair
brushed to comeliness and bright.

When she eases the door quietly open again,
almost sunrise flows through a pale ribbon.

Her robe too is loosely tied.

I slide away the sheet to make her space.
She emerges from the falling robe
as gentle and sure as the morning sun
and I become the sky waiting on the day.

joseph h. ball

THE NIGHT THE CHILDREN WERE AWAY

When she comes home he's waiting for her
    on the secluded deck, naked,
        the wine open,

her favorite cheese already sliced.
    Though he hasn't done anything
        like this in years

he knows she'll laugh at his nakedness
    as one laughs at seeing
        an old friend

at a dirty movie. Then she'll take off
    her clothes, join him.
        Tonight

he wants to make love profanely
    as if the profane
        were the only way

to disturb, to waken, the sacred.
    But neither is in a hurry.
        They sip wine,

touch a little, nothing much needs
    to be said. That glacial
        intolerable drift

toward quietude and habit, he was worried
    that he'd stopped worrying
        about it.

It's time, a kiss says, to stop time
    by owning it, transforming it
        into body-time, hip-sway

and heartbeat, though really the kiss says
    now, the now he trusts
        is both history

and this instant, reflexive, the good past
    brought forward in a rush.

stephen dunn

BEGIN IN THE NIGHT

Begin in the night,
soft rain falling,
the fingertip rain
tripping down from
the sultry sky.
Begin in the dark,
candleless lovetime,
begin your search
to find me in the dark.
Reach out, roll over,
encompass me naked,
lie here in the pool
my warmth, my sleep.
Become the music
that dances inside me,
become the bright wave
I swim into when
I close my eyes.
You are the sea in my dream,
bright sky in my morning,
your love is the wheel

that turns me toward you
and encircles my heart
with your heart.

abigail albrecht

I WANT TO LOVE YOU WITH EVERY PIECE OF THIS BODY

I want to love you with every piece of this body:
I want these strong and simple hands to divine
each delicate sound inside of you; I want
these faithful legs to gallop at midnight
through the sleeping orchards of your heart;
I want these eyes, these singing eyes
that have survived the brutal clocks, the days
lost in daily space, to blossom in some high bed
of human heaven; I want these feet that never sleep
to wander in the deepest part of you, like ghosts
unchained, ecstatic in this desert sea;
I want this blood, this red tenderness,
to be your blanket; I want this brown and peasant face
to race through solitude and rock, until
with you at last *The Book of Moon* is read;
I want this tongue, that like some acrobat insane
tumbles toward you with what little words I have,
to sip some virgin secret that you hold;
I want this heart, in time both infinite and now,
to know the reason for the light in you that lifts me.

james tipton

AUBADE

Sun-baked all day, the south-facing cliffs
breathe fire. The canyon air itself
can't sleep, sheets beneath them
gone incrementally to musk, and the man
at last awakened alone, a train whistle
moaning upriver. Maybe the train's
clank and ratchet brought her out first,
or the hope some breeze has happened,
not fire and water, the river's ice, a clammy flank of air.
Whatever it was, now the moonlight's made of her
a woman burnished by silver, leaned against the
    porch rail
and looking at the water through the almost-dark.
It's me, he says from the doorway,
and she doesn't turn, but opens
her stance, so that he might kneel
and crane his neck, and lick
along and up the sweet, salt seam
to her spine, her shoulders, her neck,
his hands a fingery wind along her arms,
down the fine column of ribs to the palm-fitted
    handles
her pelvic bones afford—

Lord, he prays, if I have sworn
my loathing for the sun and cursed the salt
that blinds my eyes at work; if I have not slept
but have believed hell a canyon of basalt
a cold clear river taunts through; if I have turned,
scalded by this skin and the murk of damp bedding,
then wake me, wake me by whatever light is called for,
so I might find her, bathed
in a glow that is pure hell alone,
but tempered by her silver
to a dark the mouths remember, breathing
flesh into flames. Let us be candles
melted to a single wax. Let us be tangled at dawn
and lick awake the lids of each other's salty eyes
and rise—

to welcome the daily fire.

robert wrigley

PART 2

self-awareness & discovery

"Now the heart sings..."

THE KISS

My mouth blooms like a cut.
I've been wronged all year, tedious
nights, nothing but rough elbows in them
and delicate boxes of Kleenex calling *crybaby
crybaby, you fool!*

Before today my body was useless.
Now it's tearing at its square corners.
It's tearing old Mary's garments off, knot by knot
and see—Now it's shot full of these electric bolts.
Zing! A resurrection!

Once it was a boat, quite wooden
and with no business, no salt water under it
and in need of some paint. It was no more
than a group of boards. But you hoisted her,
    rigged her.
She's been elected.

My nerves are turned on. I hear them like
musical instruments. Where there was silence

the drums, the strings are incurably playing. You
    did this.
Pure genius at work. Darling, the composer has
    stepped
into fire.

anne sexton

ENTRY OCTOBER 26

                    My heart swells . . . bulges—
my heart presses against my lungs, I cannot
    breathe, it rises to my throat
and throttles my words—
O it will burst sky-high surely and a cloud of star-
    lings will fly out!
A swarm of luminous moths . . . and boisterous
    starlings!

Why do they stare at me as I stride the Village streets,
crossing the crossings against the lights and
    recognizing no one?

Are my eyes too bright? Is my head too high?
Or does it really show, that kiss—does it sit on my
    lips like a moth
on a leaf, has your kiss blossomed on my mouth
    into a scarlet flower?

walter benton

BACCHANALIA

I lie
before you soaked
in white orchid, its redolence
assails like devil's fire. And when
you sheathe my body
with your flame, I get drunk
from the blood of you the flesh of you.
Then, when the new moon mounts
black sky, I inhale your breath
and pray to you: Swallow me
alive.

j. b. bernstein

I CANNOT FORGET THE WOMAN IN THE MIRROR

Backwards and upside down in the twilight, that
woman on all fours, her head
dangling and suffused, her lean
haunches, the area of darkness, the flanks and
ass narrow and pale as a deer's and those
breasts hanging down toward the center of the earth
                    like plummets, when I
swayed from side to side they swayed, it was
so dark I couldn't tell if they were gold or
plum or rose. I cannot get over her
moving toward him upside down in the mirror like a
fly on the ceiling, her head hanging down and her
tongue long and black as an anteater's
going toward his body, she was so clearly an
animal, she was an Iroquois scout creeping
naked and noiseless, and when I looked at her
she looked at me so directly, her eyes so
dark, her stare said to me I
belong here, this is mine, I am living out my
true life on this earth.

sharon olds

I love being lost
in the sound that mud makes
when it is soft and wet and begs
your fingers to stay a little while longer
and please play some more in my earth
smell this beautiful terra firma consuming you
begging you to forsake the skillful architecture of
    your hands
to make a more marvelous mess
and I love you saying look baby I have found
this branch of myself that I can use to dig
your sweet red clay to death and I say yes dig me baby
dig me as if planting love like crocuses
beneath the window of my hips.

karen garrison

LAUGHING THOROUGHBREDS

how many times
have I borne you
through the velvet night O
my thighs wrapped
tight O my thoroughbred

our small bed
vast space
where we birth
uncontrollable laughter O

my body
no longer woman
but silken flesh
on sinewy legs
galloping galloping

patti tana

THE GATEWAY

Now the heart sings with all its thousand voices
To hear this city of cells, my body, sing.
The tree through the stiff clay at long last forces
Its thin strong roots and taps the secret spring.

And the sweet waters without intermission
Climb to the tips of its green tenement;
The breasts have borne the grace of their possession,
The lips have felt the pressure of content.

Here I come home: in this expected country
They know my name and speak it with delight.
I am the dream and you my gates of entry,
The means by which I waken into light.

a. d. hope

AWAKENING

Fingers of morning sunlight
    reach across my bed.
Your touch at my shoulder,
      light as the wing of a white butterfly,
      traces curves and hollows,
      siphons passion
      to the point of skin
           on skin.

I learn the shape of my collarbone,
      awaken to wrist elbow breast and belly.
You paint smiling graffiti
      down long brown legs,
      twine curlicues
         over stretched soles.

Your hand
      trails rivulets of spindrift,
         blue and hot.
Goosebumps whisper,
    beg,
      come this way, come this way.

Silken petals unfurl,
    dark and pouting.
Your fingers
    draw my body
    shimmering and whole
        into the world.

gayle eleanor

TOUCH

My hands
open the curtains of your being
clothe you in a further nudity
uncover the bodies of your body
My hands
invent another body for your body

octavio paz

—translated from the Spanish by Charles Tomlinson

FULL SUMMER

I paused, and paused, over your body,
to feel the current of desire pull
and pull through me. Our hair was still wet,
mine like knotted wrack, it fell
across you as I paused, a soaked coil
around your glans. When one of your hairs
dried, it lifted like a bare nerve.
On the beach, above us, a cloud had appeared
in the clear air, a clockwise loop
coming in out of nothing, now the skin of
        your scrotum
moved like a live being, an animal,
I began to lick you, the foreskin lightly
stuck in one spot, like a petal, I love
to free it—just so—in joy,
and to sip from the little crying lips
at the tip. Then there was no more pausing,
nor was this the taker,
some new one came
and sucked, and up from where I had been hiding
        I was

drawn in a heavy spiral out of matter
over into another world
I had thought I would have to die to reach.

sharon olds

COMING TOGETHER

Drenched in summer sweat, I beg,
Wait, don't come yet.
The candle burned to its wick.
The heat and humidity compare
to the intensity of our want:
fire inside and out.
Your face contorts with pleasure—
we know we are near the end, spent,
but still I beg, *Wait for me,*
as I rush to catch up.
My greedy tongue travels your body
like the child I was among the dunes
of the Cape—mysterious, wild, free.
I wonder how the people beyond these walls
can sleep knowing the pleasure
their bodies contain as you scream
Yes!—More!—Harder!—Faster!—God!
until the moment—like two runners
neck and neck at the end of their race—
I demand *now* and we cross
the finish line as one, come together,
trembling, out of breath.
The wick flickers to its end

and the room goes completely black.
I say I love you, but already
you are asleep, your wet back turned
to me, so I roll to the opposite side
of the bed, find comfort in the cool
wall as I trace old, dried veins of paint
with my thumb. I do not need
to be next to you to know you love me—
it is in the numb joy of my tongue,
the ache of my hip, the pulse beneath
my nipples that recalls your lips.

jeff walt

THE WATER CYCLE

You kissed my body to a cloud—
Stratus, cirrus, nimbus,
Gasses swirling,
Furniture for angels,
Punctuation in the changing
Sentence of the sky.
Blown and altered
By the winds of breath,
I float above the landscape
Of our bed.
First cumulo-nimbus,
Then a castle of cumulo-pileus.
I expand, surround you,
Filled with dust and seas,
A plane, a bird,
Turbulence and hail.
I fill with dew.
Light shines through me,
And the earth brightens.

alison stone

TOUCHES

The sesame oil
you brought for me
to knead into your skin
makes it glisten
in the firelight.

I want to be chaste
and slow with you
now, touching circles
from your pulse points,
calling the blood up
to your surface,
using my hands to bring
ease to your body

hidden here
and there by
a vermilion edge
of quilt.

The sound you make
is new to me and I
think of the sound high

tide makes at the moment
it yields to the ebb
current, a sighing of sea
water under the tug
of a quarter moon.

I do not break
touch,
pouring more oil
into the cup
of my palm, knuckles
still to your spine

and realize
it is you
who touches me,

who anoints the dry
places, touching somewhere
nothing
has touched before.

floyd skloot

IN THE KITCHEN

Tracking you down in the kitchen
I catapult you off your feet
and simultaneously you leap into the air
and wrap your legs around my hips
gaze down on me
(those blue-green eyes with flecks of gold!)
as though I were your swing,
your trapeze,
your jaunty tightwire
taut with excitement,
and your warmth
commands my acrobatic heart
to keep on tumbling for you.
Whirling you around
I see your lips descend
to catch my lips
and feel your flying hair
electrify my neck, my face.
Gladdened, I keep whirling
and whirling
listening to the blood's applause.

alexander taylor

MAKING LOVE

We lie together and kiss many kisses:
soft pecks, sensual touching of lips,
a strong moist union.
I rise up, lift her chin, brush kisses
across her shoulder and up her neck,
her soft down hair rises in goose bumps to meet
    my lips.
She closes her eyes. I kiss her eyelids and cheek
before returning to a soft joining of lips. There we
    linger.
Sometimes she breaks to a nibble.
I join her as we pluck at one another's lips,
then open kisses, long and deep, tongues touching,
penetrating and retreating, returning to nibble,
and again going deep, searching for the soul.
All the while my hands move, exploring with
    caresses,
mapping out contour of waist and hip,
swell of buttocks, smoothness of back and curve of
    breast.
On the dresser, a clock ticks out the passing of time.
For us, in our universe,
there is only the present—it is our total existence.

My hand reaches for her breast,
feels its smoothness and follows the rising swell
to find her nipple already erect,
my finger stirs it and her passion in slow circles.
With our lips and tongues still joined,
her hand embraces my turgid penis,
teases it with the lightest touch,
discovers glistening drops of my anticipation at its
    tip.
I break the long kiss, dropping short ones
down her neck and across her breast,
my tongue captures and circles her nipple
going round and round as in some childhood game.
My hand, now free, moves down
fingers passing through curly hair
to below the mound, finding her cleft,
tracing it down to find and bring her own moisture
back to the swollen elusive pleasure spot
where my fingers, like my tongue above,
begin a movement of circular play,
moving round and round while pushing down.
Her hand tightens, squeezing my penis.
She moans, her breathing changes.
Her breath binds my hand to its rhythm—
as it quickens, my movements quicken.
She cries out.

I continue. Her pleasure continues.
There is no time but now—
with now becoming eternity.

walt farran

AFTER NEW HAMPSHIRE

Folded into each other,
origami hearts, love
knots. Each time
I never believe
we will get any closer.
Afternoon lowers
her eyes as dusk
steals across the vision
of us, still touching.
Silk light.
Silk laughter.
My body floods
its boundaries.
You hold me through
each shudder, each
moan, my head tucked
into your chest, my legs
wrapped around your body,
my body filled with light,
my body light. Past
freedom and individuality
and the delight of my own
opinions, beyond serenity

and rock 'n' roll, there is
happiness and I have found
its natural habitat beneath
your kiss and only
in your arms.

rosemary klein

ON ENTERING THE SEA

Love happened at last,
And we entered God's paradise,
Sliding
Under the skin of the water
Like fish.
We saw the precious pearls of the sea
And were amazed.
Love happened at last
Without intimidation ... with symmetry of wish.
So I gave ... and you gave
And we were fair.
It happened with marvelous ease
Like writing with jasmine water,
Like a spring flowing from the ground.

nizar qabbani

—translated from the Arabic by Lena Jayyusi and Sharif Elmusa

Spring overall. But inside us
there's another unity.

Behind each eye here,
one glowing weather.

Every forest branch moves differently
in the breeze, but as they sway
they connect at the roots.

jelaluddin rumi

—translated from the Persian by Coleman Barks
   with A. J. Arberry

PART 3

admiration & appreciation

"The wealth of you beside me..."

THE FIRST TIME EVER I SAW YOUR FACE

The first time ever I saw your face,
I thought the sun rose in your eyes,
And the moon and stars were the gift you gave
To the dark and empty skies, my love,
To the dark and empty skies.

The first time ever I kissed your mouth,
I felt the earth move in my hand,
Like the trembling heart of a captive bird
That was there at my command, my love,
That was there at my command.

The first time ever I lay with you
And felt your heart beat close to mine,
I thought our joy would fill the earth
And last till the end of time, my love,
And last till the end of time.

ewan mac coll

THE TENTH KISS

Kisses that stir my soul have no categories.
I love the wet kissing of your wet lips
but the friction of your dry little mouthing makes
smoke in my very bones, a fluid fire.
To press my lips on fluttering eyes is sweet
revenge for the torment of those butterfly kisses.
I love to lie all over you, to kiss it
all, cheeks and shoulders and neck and snowy
valleys and leave my signatures in the snow,
blue on the white dazzle of hills and valleys,
or suck with moaning mouth the tremulous tongue
that licks my own, our souls diffusing into
the strangeness of each other's flesh, soul-kissing
while love lies limp and dying of ecstasy.
Short or long or tense or loose these kisses
take me, my love, whether I'm the giver or you;
but don't let yours simply echo mine, let's play
variations for diverse instruments
and the first who fails to vary the melody
agree with shamestruck eyes to give the winner

a solo performance of all the lyrical kisses
that have come before. With all the variations.

joannes secundus

—translated from the Latin by F. X. Mathews

BONES

> "... the stony bone that can't be bribed,
> the sad bone that never gets any love...."

—*Vicente Aleixandre*
  (translated by Lewis Hyde)

Today, dear one, I attempt the impossible:
I'm going to love your bones,
I mean love your bones so they will know
that they've been loved, so your flesh
will simmer with jealousy, melt and merge
with your bones, be one with your bones
and know how cold your bones have been
without love. Are you ready? Can we do this?

It may not be easy, it may be that bones
remain without love for their own good,
it may be they can't withstand
the pressures of love, the infectious heat
of love, it may be that bones can only make it
with the hard mouth of Death. Nevertheless
today I'm going to love your bones,
beginning, of course, with your flesh....

roger pfingston

THE NINTH SECRET POEM

I worship your fleece which is the perfect triangle
    Of the Goddess
I am the lumberjack of the only virgin forest
    O my Eldorado
I am the only fish in your voluptuous ocean
    You my lovely Siren
I am the climber on your snowy mountains
    O my whitest Alp
I am the heavenly archer of your beautiful mouth
    O my darling quiver
I am the hauler of your midnight hair
    O lovely ship on the canal of my kisses
And the lilies of your arms are beckoning me
    O my summer garden
The fruits of your breast are ripening their honey for me
    O my sweet-smelling orchard
And I am raising you O Madeleine O my beauty
        above the earth
    Like the torch of all light

guillaume apollinaire

—translated from the French by Oliver Bernard

THE SHAPE OF BRIGHTNESS

If I say I helped myself to you
I hope you don't mind,
I couldn't resist;
you were just brilliant flesh—
the shape of brightness, illumined in the light of
half turned louvers that created
painted hills and valleys
with your body.

Deep sienna you were beneath me,
my skin was scorched by your sun . . .

I revelled in it;
heard the cicadas
when they made a love song,
tasted the desert sand
when I kissed you,
dreamed dreams of the Serengeti
when you stoked the fire;
and then,
I burned.

laura k. gourlay

THE SMALLEST BLUE VEINS

In my dreams no one is ever naked
or the slightest bit interested. In yours
Mel Gibson undresses you with his teeth.
I'm never rich or famous but usually
sitting in a chair or eating a bagel.
I do human things like walk down streets,
look in windows, play cards, read a book.
I'm never trapped in an elevator with anyone
but myself while you say last night
you held an umbrella on the high wire
dressed like Mata Hari. Maybe I don't
remember the gems, afraid real life
will be too boring; but how can it be, when
I wake beside you, regardless of what
I've dreamed, and see your twisted vines
of hair, corded neck, elegant throat,
each lax muscle of your naked flesh,
pelvic curve as you lie on your side,
and on the pillow, the smallest blue veins
on the back of one of your hands.

neil carpathios

LIGHTNING AT REST

Stretched out,
stone made of noon,
half-open eyes whose whiteness turns to blue,
half-ready smile.
Your body rouses, you shake your lion's mane.
Again lying down,
a fine striation of lava in the rock,
a sleeping ray of light.
And while you sleep I stroke you, I polish you,
slim axe,
arrow with whom I set the night on fire.

The sea fighting far off with its swords and feathers.

octavio paz

—translated from the Spanish by Muriel Rukeyser

THE OUTPOURING

It's the wetness I like.

The way
your pores give birth
to glittering salty beads
that sprout
about your forehead
and run
down your cheeks.
Tiny, clinging waterfalls.

The way
their adhesive
yields
as I unwrap you,
each part of your blouse
peeling
like sections of a moist
tomato skin.

The way more beads
grease our kissing bellies,
letting them slap and slide

like rapids on rocks
in a river
pounding its path
to the sea.

david meuel

BIO LOGOS

I love your face when we are making love,
like the living stones I was shocked to find
are plants, succulents, members of
a live species, although they look like blind
unblinking pebbles, unleaved, ungreen,
and ungrown. They were as unknown
to me as your face is now beside me

        —for
we have gotten ourselves in a love koan
as if we were a Japanese print born
up through Western life, torsos aslant, but
legs lifted (will we ever again find
a position so side by side?)

       —your brows cut
into angles unknown to me, eyes green
above the brown mouth's living O, a species find.

molly peacock

ON A NIGHT OF THE FULL MOON

I

Out of my flesh that hungers
and my mouth that knows
comes the shape I am seeking
for reason.
The curve of your waiting body
fits my waiting hand
your breasts warm as sunlight
your lips quick as young birds
between your thighs the sweet
sharp taste of limes.

Thus I hold you
frank in my heart's eye
in my skin's knowing
as my fingers conceive your flesh
I feel your stomach
moving against me.

Before the moon wanes again
we shall come together.

II
And I would be the moon
spoken over your beckoning flesh
breaking against reservations
beaching thought
my hands at your high tide
over and under inside you
and the passing of hungers
attended, forgotten.

Darkly risen
the moon speaks
my eyes
judging your roundness
delightful.

audre lorde

NESTING

Love outdoors,
and suddenly it is down to
one taut pine needle
flickering between your thumb
and forefinger, one green
point probing my nipple.
You want me to
tell you everything,
what feels which way,
how a nipple responds
deep in the woods
in the dark.
Upon my breast
you are weaving basketry,
holding the pine needle
in your beak as if
you are a tool-using bird.
At last you release it
and encircle
my nipple with your
spiraling tongue

and lips that
form the word
love.

abigail albrecht

WHAIA I TE PO

you have swallowed the air
of my desire that wild smell
of it down your thigh was
washed off this morning
before the toast and vegemite
i envisaged sitting round the table
with nipples for breakfast   kisses
to my backbone and of course chocolate
did you know your eyes are a
rare breed of green? and how i've gone
mad in the heart for that
sunlicked look of you
e whaiaipo
let's off to bed and play
i want to paint a love poem
all over the sheets   and you

trudi paraha

YOUR TONGUE

What a tongue
that comes out
between

your lips.
I would give
whatever you

want. I do speak
your languages:
tongue and groove,

apricot wainscoting,
butter and cream
on the kitchen table,

the one I want to
go under with you.
We will strip off

the tablecloth. We are
magicians. We make
things disappear, then

reappear, disappear, then
reappear, all night long.
But this tongue, love,

I have got to have it.
To trace the map
of my body, the inroads,

rugged terrain, back
alleys, wilderness areas.
The tip of your tongue

is the tip of a
world. I want
to see it all.

edward kleinschmidt mayes

DESCENDING

Let me take my tongue
from your mouth,
easing it out
over the red rolling
waves of your lips.
Then, let me
give it back to you,
gliding it
down
into the salty
wet canyon
between your
stiffening peaks,
down
across the tight
trembling plain
that crests and falls
with quickening pace,
down
to the swelling spring
that calls
for its caress

david meuel

HEAT IN THE BODY

I was warming your feet
with my hot breath
when I noticed your thighs
wanted to be kissed.
They were lying close together
like two long necks,
slightly bent. My lips
suckled the lighted horizon
where the leg meets the body,
that sensitive cleft I love to press.
I could smell your aroma
and I remembered the first time
I saw your sex,
how young it appeared,
partly seen, partly imagined
through the light hair that tufted
over it, dusky folds
opening slightly, like moth wings
spreading over moon flower.

david watts

TELL ME

Tell me what you see,
You ask as I lean
Into the center of your thighs
As though it is possible
To find words for such vision
As though the image of ripe persimmon
Held open and red to the sun
Could capture your fullness.
You want to know what I see
And I stand mute before you
Unable to find metaphor
For a life form so deliciously itself.
I see you, I say
And in that I'm saying
I see the cosmos
Travelling red and pink
Within your glistening skin.
I see atoms magnificently cohered
Into your desire.
I see the very bottom of the ocean,
Warm streams of water hidden there.
I see you, and I'm struck dumb.

There are no words in that part of me
Who joins with you there
My tongue flying blindly
Inside your universe.

carolyn flynn

I give you my tongue,
and the word it has for you,
and the pleasure it has for you
as I speak silently
to your body,
as I speak along the arc of your breast,
     through the cadence of your ribs,
     over the plain of your belly
and into the warm rain between your thighs,
into you.

My tongue speaks to your sex—
your perfect woman's body reads my lips,
draws my silent words
into you.

I listen
for your heady response
to the ancient language you have taught me
     My heart swells
when you speak my name
between your soft laughter and your sighs.

You guide me
artfully
    through the landscape you create with me,
to the nameless, hallowed place
    where no words will do.

patrick mulrooney

KISS

The lips of her vagina
kiss back
tender leaves

and moist like matutinal
dew. Take me back
there often.

corey mesler

        Sleep late, nobody cares what time it is.
Sunday morning, coffee in bed . . . then love
with coffee flavored kisses. And your tongue
    dripping honey like a ripe fig.

I have been hours awake looking at you
    lithely at rest in the free
natural way rivers bed and clouds shape.
Your bedgown gathers up your full round thighs,
    rolls over your hips.
Your breasts are snub like children's faces . . .
    and your navel deep

as a god's eye.
        Yes, your lips match your teats beautifully,
    rose and rose.
The hair of your arm's hollow and where your
    thighs meet
agree completely, being brown and soft to look at
    like a nest of field mice.
Praise be the walls that shelter you from eyes that
    are not mine!

Love, not prayers, shall be our offering this day.
We shall praise God with absolute embraces...
    our bodies shall sing Him
in His own incomparable tongue.
Prayer is humbleness, I cannot be humble
    with the wealth of you beside me.

walter benton

THE BUTTERFLY

those things
which you so laughingly call
hands are in fact two
brown butterflies fluttering
across the pleasure
they give
my body

nikki giovanni

IT

It is white
and satin,
great bolts of silken
cloth dropping down
through, into our center.
My eyes whiten, they widen
as if this feeling could be eaten
savored on the tongue of vision,
one gulp seeing feeling.
This is what it's like
to make love to him.

Not one moment
from the quiet
beginning to the clasp
of ending am I separate
from what is present
in his eyes also, between us
no skin, just this white cascading
and afterward,
laughter.

leatha kendrick

AFTERWORD

As soft as he came he is gone.
Standing naked beside the bed
with one fingertip trailing the ledge
of my shoulder, he looks down
at the gift of my shamelessness,
white-spiraled serenity,
a sweaty sprawl in the sheets.

Awed by the depth of his loving
trust, I let my hand fall
to rest on the line of his thigh,
feel that smile he's looking for
turn itself loose at the edge of my lips,
then succumb again to the pillow,
smile at his sway as he walks away,
and remembering, shiver.

I hear the splash on his back.
His soft sighs under the water
echo his earlier release.
I creep in to watch rivulets ride
his ridge of hip, slip into crevices

where his sweat and mine, joined
nectars, blend. I open the door.
He smiles and hands me the soap.

ginger murchison

2 AM

When I came with you that first time
on the floor of your office, the dirty carpet
under my back, the heel of one foot
propped on your shoulder, I went ahead
and screamed, full-throated, as loud
and as long as my body demanded,
because somewhere, in the back of my mind,
packed in the smallest neurons still capable
of thought, I remembered
we were in a warehouse district
and that no sentient being resided for miles.
Afterwards, when I could unclench
my hands and open my eyes, I looked up.
You were on your knees, your arms
stranded at your sides, so still—
the light from the crooknecked lamp
sculpting each lift and delicate twist,
the lax muscles, the smallest veins
on the backs of your hands. I saw
the ridge of each rib, the blue hollow
pulsing at your throat, all the colors
in your long blunt cut hair which hung
over your face like a raffia curtain
in some south sea island hut.

And as each bright synapse unfurled
and followed its path, I recalled
a story I'd read that explained why women
cry out when they come—that it's
the call of the conqueror, a siren howl
of possession. So I looked again
and it felt true, your whole body
seemed defeated, owned, having taken on
the aspect of a slave in shackles, the wrists
loosely bound with invisible rope.
And when you finally spoke you didn't
lift your head but simply moaned the word *god*
on an exhalation of breath—I knew then
I must be merciful, benevolent,
impossibly kind.

dorianne laux

ALICANTE

An orange on the table
Your dress on the rug
And you in my bed
Sweet present of the present
Cool of night
Warmth of my life.

jacques prévert

—translated from the French by Lawrence Ferlinghetti

GOOD

to be held all afternoon
in a big windowed room,
your small arms around me
your breath at my throat

to page the thick book
we learn upon your thighs,
to fold by fold your robe undo

your breast in my hand
your nipple stroked
between my fingers
shivering its full extent

bruce taylor

IN YOUR HANDS

I begin to grow extravagant,
like kudzu,
that rank, green weed
devouring house after house
in the South—
towards mid-day, the roof tiles
start to throw
a wavering light
back towards the sun,
and roads begin to soften,
darken,
taking your wayward tongue,
your legs, your eyes,
home to shuttered windows,
to the cool rooms
that invent themselves
slowly into life.

jane hirshfield

TEN YEARS TOGETHER

I wake to the wet of your
tongue licking me long. When
I am ready, you climb me,
your shoulders hunched above
your strained and standing arms,
your nipples hovering
like bulging alien eyes.

Later, as the cool air
glides our glistening bellies,
you ask: *How many times
has it been? A thousand? More?*
I tell you I don't know, either,
and you nod motionlessly,
nesting your cheek against my chest.

Soon, your breathing slows
and deepens. You slip from me,
sliding down to the sweating sheet.
And, just before I blanket us,

I see you as you were a thousand
times ago—your legs are shy,
yet they open wide for me.

david meuel

JUST BEFORE SEVENTY

it makes me laugh the
way you won't say it
out loud your
coy chuckle makes your thighs
quiver there around my ears the musk
of your scent thick on my tongue
while you giggle, nibble the tip of me
say it, I urge when I can tear my tongue
from the pink bounty glistening beneath,
say it, and you
giggle,
nibble between the
deep groans in your flushed throat
okay, you pant, hot breath on my
firmness, *just . . . before . . .*
seventy . . .

rusty fischer

I LOVE IT WHEN

I love it when you roll over
and lie on me in the night, your weight
steady on me as tons of water, my
lungs like a little, shut box,
the firm, haired surface of your legs
opening my legs, my heart swells
to a taut purple boxing glove and then
sometimes I love to lie there doing
nothing, my powerful arms thrown down,
bolts of muslin rippling from the selvage,
your pubic bone a pyramid set
point down on the point of another
—glistening fulcrum. Then, in the stillness,
I love to feel you grow and grow be-
tween my legs like a plant in fast motion
the way, in the auditorium, in the
dark, near the beginning of our lives,
above us, the enormous stems and flowers
unfolded in silence.

sharon olds

PART 4

union & ecstasy

"We feel the old earth spin . . ."

THE ENJOYMENT

Ye gods! the raptures of that night!
What fierce convulsions of delight!
How in each other's arms involved
We lay confounded and dissolved!
Bodies mingling, sexes blending,
Which should be most lost contending,
Darting fierce and flaming kisses,
Plunging into boundless blisses,
Our bodies and our souls on fire,
Tossed by a tempest of desire
Till with utmost fury driven
Down, at once, we sunk to heaven.

anon

CREATION

From the first,
we had designs upon each other
licked out in salty patterns
on sex-sweated skin,

I painted your body
with a curly brush of copper hair
which, at times, you smoothed
back from my face
so that we could see ourselves
in true and unveiled mirrors,

your explorer's hands followed
every fold and contour
of my entire landscape, out and in,
causing me to liquify making you
a happy child again
with secret, candy-sticky fingers,

as my softness hardened you,
your stiffness melted me until
I,
    dripping around you and
you,
    deeply dipping inside me
found an undiscovered world
of land and water,

awakened and alive with wonder,
we created a sculpture
    shimmering with love.

dara prisamt murray

PUBLIC AFFECTION

when he kisses her/ when
lips meet/ the winds
still/ to stop/ and
watch/ and stare
transfixed/ something
a breeze rarely does.
the birds quiet
their song/ cock an
invisible ear/ so they
can hear
wetness pass between
mouths/ a soft
song/ more soothing
than theirs.
the sun brightens its light
so all can see/ and cools its heat
to make space for the fire
burning/ heat generating
between two small people

on planet earth.
must be magic/ to stir
the wind's curiosity
and quiet the bird's song.

emani

I flung closer to his breast,
As sword that, after battle, flings to sheath;
And, in that hurtle of united souls,
The mystic motions which in common moods
Are shut beyond our sense, broke in on us,
And, as we sate, we felt the old earth spin,
And all the starry turbulence of worlds
Swing round us in their audient circles, till,
If that same golden moon were overhead
Or if beneath our feet, we did not know.

elizabeth barrett browning

—from "Aurora Leigh"

LOVE POEM

From here those slaps of color unravel
form you said and stepped back
from the Monet to see the separate strokes
fall into water and lilies again.
Shards of light take the eye to blossoms
pale as breasts. Sky, leaf, water, flower
merge and waver, blur then clear
as each takes something from the other
to reflect or repeat so that not a single
moment is preserved but several.

Later in the splay of late afternoon
we repeat that painting.
The spread blooms of our bodies
blend and shift and merge again until
we know as Monet knew in the crystal rush
of water over the sun-glazed lilies
the radiance of an instant.

sarah brown weitzman

IN THE ABSENCE OF OCEAN

In the absence of ocean
I wash myself in the salt of your body,
whether arching up and up to meet you
as you ride above me, intent as a swimmer
cresting a wave, or lowering myself
upon your surge and swell, as open
to possibility as the sea cave
I discovered and swam in as a child.

It is the most ancient of movements,
this rising, breaking, and falling
that moves through us like water, simple
as our bodies which are so largely salt.
But I had not thought to know it again,
the small boat of my life broken up,
broken into, everything familiar
smashed to pieces against the rocks.

It was all wind-chop and ice-swirl
and I was barely surviving, treading
the fathomless dark, fighting the currents,
forgetting the lesson of surrender undulating
in the lift and sway of kelp.

Then you were there and recalled
something of the ocean inside me
as I recalled something of the ocean
in you—how the salt helps heal us
even as it stings, tears welling
unexpectedly in my eyes
as your lashes quiver
and your breath comes quickly
in short, shallow gasps
that are somehow mine too

as we move together
like wind upon water,
like sea grass or dolphins,
the divine surge
and current of swell
blessing us, making us whole.

alison townsend

AT THE KITCHEN COUNTER

At the kitchen counter, cooking
talking of our love,
the loves that hadn't worked before.

Onion waxed translucent
in butter and olive oil;
grains of rice, wine and broth
risotto plumping, concentrating on the stove—

we taste asparagus and mushrooms
drink Alsatian Reisling
look into each other's eyes
and know this time there is a difference
in this love that we can taste and chew—
this love will nurture us.

We reach across the plates and glasses
sparks arc between our finger tips—
we have to have each other for dessert.

After, back in the kitchen,
you call me to you,
unfold your robe

and draw my hand into our wetness—
I fall onto my knees to worship
and to taste of it.

And in the night,
weaving in and out of sleep,
in and out of consciousness—
every time to find you
folded in my arms—
wrapped up like a present
we are giving to each other.

jay farbstein

WET

Desire urges us on deeper
and farther into the coral maze
of the body, dense, tropical
where we cannot tell plant
from animal, mind from body
prey from predator, swaying
magenta, teal, green-golden
anemones weaving wide open.

The stronger lusts flash
corn rows of dagger teeth,
but the little desires slip,
sleek frisky neon flowers
into the corners of the eye.
The mouth tastes their strange
sweet and salty blood
burning the back of the tongue.

Deeper and deeper into
the thick warm translucence
where mind and body melt,
where we see with our tongues
and taste with our fingers;

there the horizon of excess
folds as we approach
into plains of not enough.

Now we are returned to ourselves
flung out on the beach
exhausted, flanks heaving
out of oxygen and time,
grinning like childish daubs
of boats. Now it is sleep
draws us down, surrendered
to its dark glimmer.

marge piercy

OH YEAH

be great to get you in a feather bed
in the middle of the afternoon
fifties jazz running through my head

like a pair of eager newlyweds
completely unzipped, unbuttoned, undone
be great to get you in a feather bed

bared to the bone, nothing unsaid
coltrane's celestial saxophone
fifties jazz running through my head

jamming with you as the sky turns red
then dark to black and then the moon—
be great to get you in a feather bed

your cultured lips could wake the dead
the wetted reed beneath your tongue
fifties jazz running through my head

the familiar tune worn, smoothed and ragged
the sweet high wail that turns to moan
be great to fuck you in a feather bed
fifties jazz running through my head

charles rossiter

SPILLING

tongue his moan cherry

dew drop slop and merry

sluice   we sex

and spilling (this

is thrilling)

stars all through

the bed

a nectar laden   petal spread

now

he with fingers

(cunning)   lingers

ah deep sighs

a toast to your green eyes

shivery hips and

easy   gentle   jut o slips

inside

sweaty salty yes let's ride

and pant and hollering with glee

a c........c......cuming is She

trudi paraha

OCCASION

We wake entangled,
leg over leg,
frightened out
of darkness by light
that would not burn
an hour ago in wind
and storm. Five a.m.
tolls like a buoy.
Naked, I rise
grotesquely shadowed
to kill the glare.
Something remembered
(the promise of
morning love?)
brings me down again,
my hand between
your thighs carving a
sweet red wound.
Your breasts float up
to meet my hands
and lips. We crawl
through each other
and back again

guided by our blood-
electric finger tips.
I swim in you,
you in me until we
drift down, slowly
settling in anemone
of pillowed hair,
entangled leg and arm,
beneath our tongues
a dream of fruit,
tide of sunlight
inching over the dark
planetary coast.

roger pfingston

HORIZONS

Last night your body
was a rosebush,

The thorn of your love
rising and falling.

We've been together
for so long,

We curl in an opening
in a leaf on the world's tree.

We root where the wind carried us,
in a crack in a rock of the world.

A thorn the axis
of the world's wheel turning—

A buzz rises around us,
a cloud of wings beating the air.

Another blossom opens
around our blossoming,

Another horizon joins
the simple horizon of two bodies.

barbara la morticella

AXIS

Through the conduits of blood
my body in your body
           spring of night
my tongue of sun in your forest
             your body a kneading trough
I red wheat
        Through the conduits of bone
I night I water
          I forest that moves forward
I tongue
     I body
       I sun-bone
Through the conduits of night
            spring of bodies
You night of wheat
         you forest in the sun
you waiting water
         you kneading trough of bones
Through the conduits of sun
           my night in your night
my sun in your sun
          my wheat in your kneading trough

your forest in my tongue
                 Through the conduits of the body
water in the night
             your body in my body
Spring of bones
           Spring of suns

octavio paz

—translated from the Spanish by Eliot Weinberger

GRAVITY

When you step away
        For a moment alone
In another room
        Your warmth lingers
On my fingers and palms
        On my mouth.

No matter how quick
        Your return
An eternity passes
        While at my core
A lava flow pulses
        Seeking release.
I marvel at need
        Still so great
We've done this
        A thousand times
At least.

When you return
        With quick steps
I'm at the bedroom door
        Our mouths meet

You turn in my embrace
    My touch is everywhere
And yours as well
    Our clothes fall
And we fall onto
    Into each other
A wondrous letting go
    That is always new.

rick fournier

ALL YEAR LONG

1

We break off a branch of poplar catkins.
A hundred birds sing in the tree.
Lying beneath it in the garden,
We talk to each other,
Our tongues in each other's mouth.

2

The sultry air is heavy with flower perfumes.
What is there better to do this hot night
Than throw off the covers
And lie together naked?

3

A cold wind blows open the window.
The moon looks in, full and bright.
Not a sound,
Not a voice,
In the night.
Then from behind the bed curtains,
Two giggles.

4

A freezing sky.
The year ends.
Icy winds whirl the snowflakes.
Under the covers
My darling is hotter than midsummer night.

anonymous

—translated from the Chinese by Kenneth Rexroth

CORNFIELD

This wide bed is our cornfield,
fallow and blanket-green,
you and I its farmers.

In the winter of our desire
the winds of our words
rattle the dried leaves
left on the stalks.
The land sleeps,
and we sleep in it,
separately, like tramps
who are nowhere else welcome.

When the new breezes wake us
to the spring's duties, we seed
the field with the sureness of love,
and with the summer heat
the passionate corn ripens
beneath its green veiling,
our cries echoing
like those of the crows.

gail morse

ALL THAT WET

All that sweat when you come in
from mowing the lawn.
Music, loud music, overflows the house.
I'm drenched too, from washing
windows in 90 degree heat.
You slip your arms around me
and pick up the beat.
Your lips on mine so quick.
Fish, we're fish,
as we swish, dancing circles on the tile floor.
Kisses wide and wet.
Ah, but fish have no tongues.
My bare feet scale up the beat.
Your hands slip
the curve of my back and hip.
Lightly I run out the line of your arm,
(Are you playing me or am I baiting you?)
twist back again.
Dive with me, I sigh throaty and low,
wiggle against you enticingly slow.
You, the salt lick and motion.
We reel with the rip and tide of ocean.

diane quintrall lewis

O It's Nice To Get Up In,the slipshod mucous kiss
of her riant belly's fooling bore
—When The Sun Begins To(with a phrasing crease
of hot subliminal lips,as if a score
of youngest angels suddenly should stretch neat necks
just to see how always squirms
the skilful mystery of Hell)me suddenly

grips in chuckles of supreme sex.

In The Good Old Summer Time.
My gorgeous bullet in tickling intuitive flight
aches,just,simply,into,her.   Thirsty
stirring.   (Must be summer.   Hush.   Worms.)
But It's Nicer To Lie In Bed
      —eh?   I'm

not.   Again.   Hush.   God.   Please hold.   Tight

e. e. cummings

AND SUNDAY MORNING

All day in a daze of your making
of our making / love-making
all day awake / to the sleep / of the ship
of the under-cover lover / the above-board sprawl
all day in the daze / of the laze / of us both
in the puckered nipple / and the salt expanse
all day in the thigh / in the sly eye
of the belly-button / in the curve of your flank
in the laughing moustache of my own pubic hair
all day in the nimbus / the haze
in the cloud of the sound / of the mosquito buzz
of our love

christian mc ewen

ARMFULS OF SUMMER

In lustful
    hot undress

We celebrate
    the great black night.

With summer
    in our hair

Our bodies brim
    with fruits and meat.

We help ourselves,
    each to each.

Lean into the
    curve of my body.

What we do together
    we do

Until the rising moon
    exposes us.

Until the tide
    takes back the beach.

kathleen iddings

APRICOTS AND FIGS

"*If love be not in the house there is nothing.*"
—*Ezra Pound*

The wind through the fine wire screen
scatters finely over us who only seem
to mind. Like wild ribbons we have wrapped
each other's bodies in this room, cream-
and chocolate-colored, on this bed, draped
like a fountain, centered in us. We have seen
what thickness love is. We have climbed ladders
to touch the young figs and be touched by them.
The tree shakes, this one apricot, and scatters
fruit. All stars come out in trees and every stem
is heavy with confusion of itself attached, then
unattached and free. The fig loves the apricot.
More of each come showering the bed, all opened
and flaming with a delight that never stops.

edward kleinschmidt mayes

THIS NIGHT ONLY

[*ERIC SATIE:* GYMNOPÉDIE #1]

Moonlight   now   on Malibu
The winter night   the few stars
Far away   millions   of miles
The sea   going on   and on
Forever   around   the earth
Far   and   far   as your lips   are near
Filled   with the same light   as your eyes
Darling   darling   darling
The future   is long gone by
And the past   will never happen
We have   only this
Our one forever
So small   so infinite
So brief   so vast
Immortal   as our hands that touch
Deathless   as the firelit wine we drink
Almighty   as this single kiss
That has no beginning
That will never
Never
End

kenneth rexroth

SWANS' SONG

The snowflakes flutter down outside our bed-
room window; framing you, neck bent, outstretched
toward me. The silver down upon your breast
holds the winter air at bay. I press
my lips deep into your plumes, onto the silky,
skin that leaps for me. My fingers trace
the history in the lines etched on your cheek;
your tongue re-paints the stretch marks on my hip.

You'll glide along me like a swan upon
its own reflection, skimming sheets, and toss-
ing among the pillow swells. The mattress
crests, spraying memories locked inside
the creaking springs—a broken bag
of waters, milk spilled from a newborn's lips,
a thousand fevers' beads of sweat, the sweet
strawberry stain of our May wedding night.

Through the foam of this thick and ancient
lake, we'll propel ourselves along;

our undulating necks, those pendulums,
push us deep into the night, where our
glistening cries will pierce the dark, like stars.

elizabeth m. dalton

CLOUDBURST

Red wine like dripping rubies in a glass;
Soft skin like liquid pearls around your waist.
Green eyes like glowing boats still slowly pass,
Through night, like sprinkled darkness we can taste.
The future waits neglected up ahead.
The past, a silent shadow on a shore;
Our perfect presence pulses through our bed,
As still air sings the quenched and quiet score.
The breath of everything is damp and warm,
And nothing needs to know itself at all.
The crackling clouds begin to burst then swarm,
Across the sky. The drops begin to fall.
Soaking us in laughter without measure,
Rise, and float away on teeming pleasure.

ed l. wier

NIGHT OF BLUE STARS

You come to me in the sequined darkness
the weighted darkness of our secret garden
the candled night melts its luminous fingers
as the dark sky paints you blue

I reach you in torrents of honeyed wine
I reach you in a rush of spilled seawater
I cling to you wrapped in strong vines and red flowers
in the glinting night of blue stars

abigail albrecht

THE NIGHT

Just as paint seems to leap from the paintbrush
to clapboards that have gone many years unpainted
and disappear into them almost with a slurp,
so their words, as they lie and talk, their faces
almost touching, jump from one mouth to the other
without apparent sound except little lip-wetting
        smacks.
When their mouths touch at last they linger, making
small eating motions and suction squeaks.
She licks three slithery syllables on his chest,
looks up, smiles, shines him the same three.
In his gasps suspense and gratefulness mix,
as in the crinkling unwrapping of Christmas
        packages.
Where he touches her she glisses smooth and shining
as the lower lip of a baby tantalizing its gruel bowl
with lengthening and shortening dangles of drool.
Her moans come with a slight delay, as if the
        sequence
happens across a valley, the touch and then the cry.
Their bones almost hit—the purpose of flesh
may be to keep the skeletons from bruising each
        other.

One of them calls out in cackling, chaotic rattles,
like a straw suddenly sucking the bottom. Then,
        with a sound
like last bathwater seized by the Coriolis force,
the other calls out. They lie holding each other.
For a moment the glue joining body and soul does
        not ache.
They are here and not here, like the zebra,
whose flesh has been sliced up and reassembled
in alternating layers with matter from elsewhere.
The sense that each one had of being divided in two
has given way to the knowledge that each is half
of the whole limb-tangle appearing like a large
altricial hatchling occupying much of the bed.
The man squinches himself up against the back
of the woman, an arm crooks over her waist,
his hand touches sometimes her hand, sometimes
        her breast,
his penis settles along the groove between her
        buttocks,
falls into deep sleep, almost starts to snore.
If someone were to discover them this way,
him like the big, folded wings of her,
they might stay as they are, the way the woodcock,
believing herself safe in her camouflage, sometimes
sits still until a person stoops and reaches out to
        pet her—

then jumps six feet straight up and wherries off.
When the sun enters the room, he wakes and
    watches her.
Her hair lies loose, strewn across the pillow
as if it has been washed up, her lips are blubbed,
from the kissing, her profile is fierce,
like that of a figurehead seeing over
the rim of the world. She wakes.
They do not get up yet. It is not easy
to straighten out bodies that have been lying
all night in the same curve, like two paintbrushes
wintering in a coffee can of evaporated turpentine.
They hear the clangs of a church clock. Why only
    nine?
When they have been lying on this bed since before
    the earth began.

galway kinnell

PART 5

afterglow & remembrance

"Eternity is this moment..."

SOMETIMES, AFTER MAKING LOVE

Sometimes, after making love, when
we lie in the lavender silence
and feel the blood slip
through our arteries and veins,
sliding through the capillaries, thin as
root hairs, bringing bliss to the most
remote outposts of our bodies, delivering
oxygen and proteins, minerals, all the rich
chemicals our cells crave and devour
as we have devoured each other, I
lie there as sound reasserts itself,
and listen to the soft ticking of the clock
and a foghorn, faint from the lighthouse,
a car door slams across the street,
and I want to say something to you,
but it's like trying to tell a dream,
when the words come out flat as
handkerchiefs under the iron and the listener
smiles pleasantly like a person who doesn't
speak the language and nods at everything.
It should be enough that we have
lived these hours, breathing
each other's breath, catching it like

wind in the sails of our bodies.
It should be enough. And yet
I carry the need for speech, strung
on the filaments of my DNA like black pearls,
from the earliest times when
our ancestors must have lain still,
like us, in amazement
and groped for the first words.

ellen bass

WHERE I GO AFTER SEX

I won't tell you this is a memory.
You won't ever know I'm on a country
road after rain, water-logged birds
shaking their wings, globs of water

flopping from tree branches, scattered
puddles of half-formed reflection,
some I step over, others I splash my way
through. You'll think it's just our

bodies climbing down from all that
passion, the sweat of it now seeping
from our pores whiter than light.
You won't see the heavy petals

of the bluebells or the huddled cache
of monarchs slowly splitting into
single butterflies. You'll feel my thigh
like a ribbon draped down yours.

You'll roam my chest with gentler
fingers, as if the ribs are not May
hills, the nipples some place other than
fluttering on a thousand drying branches.

.

You'll whisper words of love like
they're coming from you while I'll
say mine to the wet grass I kneel into,
to the root of a wild flower I nudge

up from the muddy soil as if to hand
its beauty back to someone. The clouds
are breaking, It's for you. The sun is
shining and again I thank you for it.

john grey

AFTERWARDS

when we sat side by side
on the edge of the unmade bed,
staring blindly at our knees, our feet,
our clothes stranded in the middle of the floor
like small, crumpled islands,
you put your arm around my shoulder
in that gesture usually reserved
for those of the same sex—equals,
friends, as if we'd
accomplished something together,
like climbing a hill or painting a house,
your hand at rest over the curved bone
of my shoulder, my loud nipples
softening into sleep.
Stripped of our want, our wildness, we sat
naked and tired and companionable
in the sleek silence, innocent
of what we'd said, what we'd done,
our breath slowing, our heads tipped
and touching at the crown,
like a couple of kids

slumped on a dock in the sun, our legs
dangling above the bright water,
admiring each other's reflections.

dorianne laux

A GOOD AFTERNOON

Your legs wide open after love,
we fall back tasting each other.

Or is it the peach, whose other half
still glistens on the windowsill?

roger pfingston

SUN AND MOON

It's all about sex,
we both know that.

But   what I wonder is
why
after every molecule of desire
in my body has been satisfied
after
the sudden moistening, the deep
fierce aching and rising heat,
after
the throbbing glory of release and the cries
of need and pleasure have dissolved
into the air,

Something like my soul slips from me
and goes to you,
without choice or question,
and wraps itself around you
all night, like the breath
of the moon

And why
I carry the thought of you
as constant as any sun
in my heart.

gina zeitlin

LOVE & DESIRE

Falling up into the sky.
To swim fishlike and prone through the dazzle,
and me, the smallest speck, only a shimmer of reason
leaning in toward the point of consent.
But you, there: what a constellation!
The whole music welling up, prismatic and infinite.

If there were more than this, what language could
       hold us?
or what fine cilia on the belly of desire?
The mouth itself might be a place of wisdom,
the tongue a monument to progress,
the lips, each one a citadel cast open like the first
       day in May.
And the teeth? Once barriers to communion, they
       now each sing
like the blue green waves, rising on their backs
and arched for pleasure
as the curl of foam takes them by surprise.

Joining in as many ways and grateful.
Even my hair this morning is glad.

And the sky, who sometimes has her reasons,
comes down gently all around us,
touching her blue hem to every particular
until the whole cake rises in the sun!

elizabeth claman

FIRE

Hear the spit and crack
of kindling. We melt
together like flames.
Sparks fly from our mouths.
Cool blue-green flames
enclose us, a lagoon.

In pewter moonlight
let the house set sail,
lit by embers.
While I sleep, love,
bring me incense and gold.

Your body warms me;
mist becoming rain
clatters the roof.
Tomorrow morning poke
amid ashes, touch
the lovely uncharred forms.

lucille lang day

FINISHING TOUCHES

We lie sideways
under the sheltering
sheet. I
have wedged myself
against the back
of you, my arms
wrapped
around your sides,
my hands
around your breasts.
Your hands
cover mine.

We talk
in touches now.

We listen
to each other's fingertips.

david meuel

NIGHT POEM

I lie on my back
savor aching hips
ribs that rocked their bone
against yours.
The small night wind
dries our cheeks,
plays with my wet hair.
My belly floats in it,
my soft breasts,
brown nipples dimpling,
and I am gone to mist
a handful of water our fingers spilled
rising.

penny harter

TIME TO EMBRACE

The resolute moon is framed
just above the treetops
in the narrow parting of curtains.
My eyes, startled by the full light,
open abruptly to it and to the liquid
embodiment of time—digital time—
hovering beneath the window:
2:39, in angular, red numbers.

The disorientation clears
and I am returned
to our analog time:
the big hand (mine)
on the bare swell of your hip
your small hand clutching
my shrunken, still damp
cock like a lifeline, clinging
to time that spends itself
whether we spend it or not.

While we were not looking
the dogwood faded
and is best forgotten

leaving the moment uncluttered:
the ascendant moon, lighting
your flesh as it blossoms
in its own season, comes
full like the moon
in the fullness of time.

michael foster

Her eyes in sleep
afterward

her body my love

sounds she uttered then
without meaning

yet not meaningless

my heartbeat even now
echoing them.

anonymous

—translated from the Sanskrit by W. S. Merwin
   and J. Moussaieff Masson

LISTENER

The woman with her face pressed
against my chest and both legs
locked around my knee, breathing deeply,
has floated into some quiet stream,
swaying past its wooded banks without me.

Somehow I've told her everything, whispered it
through my cracked voice
into the stillness around her
as we sat in the gloom
waiting for the movies to begin,
and later by the bridge,
watching dim surf ignite offshore.
In this bed I've exploded each grief into her body,
one by one, until they came loose:
the drinking, the failed marriages and jobs,
the weight of my children pressing me down.

There must be some kindness I could bring
to her dream now, listening to her breath
unwind in the small room
and wishing I had never hurt anyone.

What still country have I come to,
where the long grass bends under the animals
when they lie down, emptied of suffering?
What slow river flows beneath her forehead,
the petals of her ears adrift in the auburn hair,
gathering darkness?

joseph millar

MYTH

It is after love that he returns
to the quiet light of the mind. Her half asleep
in the August heat. Him understanding
the ancient myth of her legs
tangled in thin sheets but refusing
to diminish it with words. The singing
still faint in their brown bodies.
What consumes him now is the myth of lovers
long at it. Desire as it lives closer to the light.
Our knowing the signs. The dance
more complex in its suddenness.
How after swimming in the late afternoon
as he dried her back she turned to him
stunned by her need, him again
surprised when he entered her, still
carefully searching the map of her,
both of them seeking a perfection they know
doesn't exist but insisting like all lovers
again and again on its possibility.
The mystery of the sweetness never revealed.
Only more familiar. Visiting what they believe
to be godly within. Like the Buddhist monk
in the moonlight, sweeping the long stairs

year after year, believing there is more to learn
in the darkness, knowing the moon
does not begin with his heart
but stopping every so often
in the stillness of his shadow
to consider it so.

jonathan blake

SEAMLESS BEAUTY

> *"The flower, the sky, your beloved, can only be*
> *found in the present moment."*
> —*Thich Nhat Hanh*

Bittersweet, this lying under you,
your nose buried in my neck.
Can't get enough of your scent, you mumble,
and fall asleep.

I kiss the sweat-licked shiny top of your head
and twirl my finger slowly round and round
a lock of hair at the base of your neck.
Round and round, echoing the tug,
pull and swirling of our energies
which only moments ago, spun us out,
off this soft bed, careening to a place
where our joining felt infinite.

Someday I'd like to die this way
with you still inside me,
fall into a deep sleep and never wake up,
never have to know the parting,
the spent wave leaving the shore.

Your hair hugs my finger, and falls away.
Each twirl brings you closer yet farther from me.
The holding on becomes the letting go.

wendy lee

AUBADE

Stay, O sweet, and do not rise,
The light that shines comes from thine eyes;
The day breaks not, it is my heart,
Because that you and I must part.
 Stay, or else my joys will die,
 And perish in their infancy.

anon

MORNING

In the days of the lengthening of light
and the burgeoning of ivy,
on a Sunday morning, I encourage
the chartreuse intrusion of color
into our room of curtainless windows
where I lie in the space
your getting up has created in the bed,
a new book of poems beside me,
and the piquant scent our
acceleration into pleasure has left
announcing itself to liquid on my thighs.

maureen tolman flannery

REDBUD

Walking beneath
the flowering redbud,
whose purple blossoms,
you told me,
can be eaten
and taste sweet,
I am not sure
whether the fragrance
I inhale
is that of your body
remaining with mine,
and reminding me
of this morning
after an evening
of love,
or the petals
of blossoms
blown from a branch
that become a streak
of freshness
on the wind,
not unlike
the way

you have marked me,
with such sweet surfeit,
that I am yours.

wally swist

THE ORDINARY DAY BEGINS

at my desk
the screen blinks on
numbers begin their race
but inside me, the throb
of your last morning thrusts
continue, echo
you in me

the quiet seep of love spreads
I smile in secret
the computer hums
I, too, am humming, low
waves receding
washes of warm light

figures flit and flash
numbers, columns, rows,
I stare and suck my lower lip
that tastes of you,
your last kiss lingers
long after the ordinary day begins

june sylvester saraceno

LASTNIGHT, AFTER WE MADE LOVE

My hair was wild
my face, barely recognizable,
later,
in the harsh light of the
bathroom mirror.

Now,
seeing myself by the
soft afternoon,

I remember you beneath me,
your forehead damp and glistening,

your mouth, slightly open.
Then you, saying
over and over again,

You're so beautiful.
You're so beautiful...

Never leaving out the subject
of that sentence, as though I, too,
might disappear with that omission.

Pausing, each time, in between,
each time offering what
we had formed there
in the friction of our flesh.

Until, finally, the moment started
spinning off its course,
began to wobble under the weight
of its own beauty,

like a planet
having given up the
tedium of its orbit
to be pulled, suddenly,
into the sun.

danusha laméris de garza

IN VICTORIA'S SECRET, NEAR THE BRAS

The woman wants to know if I need help.
She's seen me fingering the lacy cups,
thinking of you
and those pendulous orbs
that swing above my naked nights,
that harden like stones
and fill my mouth
and box my ears
and glisten.

I should tell her
when we're spooned together,
how they pancake, flat,
against my back,
when you brush your hair
I watch them in the mirror,
barely jiggle,

how to the sweat I sucked
from each sweet nipple
still on my tongue—
to all your body's miraculous ways
that gauge all need,
I return.

And that's why I browse
like a bra junkie,
lingering what must seem
too long,
needing a fix.

neil carpathios

MAIDENHAIR AND WILD ROSES

I found the note
in the lunch
you had packed for me
that read, "I love you.
Remember this morning?"
And I did remember,
standing beneath the cliffs
partway up the mountain,
those massive mossy altars
lush with fern,
the emptiness at the center
of a frond of maidenhair,
silky with a spider's web,
and in full bloom
a pair of the reddest
wild roses, growing
from the same stem,
and, as if they could speak,
not unlike you and I
when we give voice
to passion, they spoke
in sweet declaratives,
trailing a fragrance

as rich as their color,
so thoroughly engaged
they were, as well as we,
in the language of the heart.

wally swist

A MOMENT

When we loved—
possessed by violent passion—
we knew.
We did not know.
Eternity
                is this moment.

In the deep half-sleep
it seemed as if
the harsh, tense world
suddenly grew quiet.
Even the pillows
have sunk into sleep.

Far off, as if in a dream,
echoed the words of the poet—
What is it that matters?
What is it that lasts?

abraham linik

LAST NIGHT

The next day, I am almost afraid.
Love? It was more like dragonflies
in the sun, 100 degrees at noon,
the ends of their abdomens stuck together, I
close my eyes when I remember. I hardly
knew myself, like something twisting and
twisting out of a chrysalis,
enormous, without language, all
head, all shut eyes, and the humming
like madness, the way they writhe away,
and do not leave, back, back,
away, back. Did I know you? No kiss,
no tenderness—more like killing, death-grip
holding to life, genitals
like violent hands clasped tight
barely moving, more like being closed
in a great jaw and eaten, and the screaming
I groan to remember it, and when we started
to die, then I refuse to remember,
the way a drunkard forgets. After,
you held my hands extremely hard as my
body moved in shudders like the ferry when its
axle is loosed past engagement, you kept me

sealed exactly against you, our hairlines
wet as the arc of a gateway after
a cloudburst, you secured me in your arms till I slept—
that was love, and we woke in the morning
clasped, fragrant, buoyant, that was
the morning after love.

sharon olds

ACKNOWLEDGMENTS

I am grateful to many people for their support and contributions in creating this book. In particular, I thank Felicia Eth, my longtime literary agent, for her energy and enthusiasm. From the get-go Felicia recognized the book's social value, and she expertly ferried it through the necessary steps toward publication. I am deeply grateful to Jason Gardner, my affable editor at New World Library, for his excitement and commitment to this project. In addition, I thank others at New World Library—Becky Benenate, Marc Allen, and Munro Magruder—for their continued interest, help, and assistance. I greatly appreciate having a publisher who values poetry and the lasting beauty of a well-crafted literary text.

I was aided in the development of the manuscript by two very talented people. In particular, I thank fellow anthologist, poet, and friend Elizabeth Claman for her valuable help with editing, arranging, and sequencing the works. She also provided beneficial input and wording for the introduction. Besides being fun to work with, Elizabeth shared ideas that significantly improved the presentation and power of the anthology. I am also grateful to David Meuel, a wonderful poet, who took a special interest in the project and offered assistance. He generously supplied me with a steady stream of poems culled from his personal library of love poem favorites. The feedback Elizabeth and David provided, regarding which poems they liked best and why, helped shape the final manuscript. Putting together a book can be a lonely experience. I feel blessed to have enjoyed Elizabeth's and David's interest, humor, and caring along the way.

I am also grateful to a whole community of poets and writers, many of whom appear in my first anthology, *Passionate Hearts,* for their interest and involvement in this book as well. Special thanks go to Sharon Olds, Molly Peacock, Patti Tana, Jane Hirshfield, Ellen Bass, Frank Gaspar, Galway Kinnell, Michael S. Smith, Marge Piercy, Dorianne Laux, Steve Shankman, Joyce Jenkins, Micha Grudin, and Charles Rossiter for spreading the word about the anthology and generously providing help when needed. In addition, I appreciate the many letters I received from readers who praised *Passionate Hearts* and cheered me on to do a second anthology.

A special thank you goes to Thomas Moore for his

generous involvement in reading the manuscript and writing an excellent foreword. I am deeply grateful that he took time from his busy schedule to support this project.

Many thanks go to Suzie Boss, a writer and dear friend, for providing last-minute editorial feedback and expert help with the introduction and other sections of the book. I am also grateful to my teenage daughter Cara and her friend Amber for their spontaneously crafted "Intimate Kisses" collage. It was inspiring having a well-decorated box in which to keep all the poetry submissions. In addition, I appreciate Cara for her candid reactions and comments about some of the works under consideration. I thank Ryan Kirkpatrick and Alisha Barrowcliff for research and typing assistance. And I am especially grateful to Marcella Salvi and Lauretta De Renza-Huter for helping with the Italian translation of the poem I wrote for my husband, Larry, which appears on the dedication page.

Speaking of whom, in closing, I want to thank my marvelous husband, Larry Maltz, for his love, support, intelligence, and humor. Larry patiently helped me brainstorm the organization for the anthology on one of our weekly walks along the Willamette River. And he frequently provided the male perspective and reaction I needed to create an anthology sensitive to the emotional realities of both women and men.

PERMISSIONS ACKNOWLEDGMENTS

Grateful acknowledgment is made to poets who contributed unpublished and previously published works for this collection. Unless specifically noted otherwise, copyright of the poems is held by the individual poets. Thanks also are due to the following poets, publications, and publishers for permission to reprint the copyrighted materials listed below:

VIRGINIA HAMILTON ADAIR: "Peeling an Orange," from *Ants on the Melon: A Collection of Poems* by Virginia Hamilton Adair. Copyright © 1966 by Virginia Hamilton Adair. Reprinted by permission of Random House, Inc.

ANON: "Aubade," from *Sanskrit Love Poetry,* translated by W.S. Merwin and J. Moussaieff Masson. Copyright © 1977 by Columbia University Press. Reprinted by permission of Columbia University Press.

ANON: "All Year Long," from *One Hundred More Poems from the Chinese* by Kenneth Rexroth. Copyright © 1970 by Kenneth Rexroth. Reprinted by permission of New Directions Publishing Corp.

ELLEN BASS: "Sometimes, After Making Love" appeared in *Quarry West* (Porter College, University of California, Santa Cruz), "Poets and Writers of the Monterey Bay," vol. 35/36, 1999, p. 16. Copyright © 1999 by Ellen Bass. Reprinted by permission of the author.

WALTER BENTON: "Entry October 26" and "Entry June 12" from *This Is My Beloved* by Walter Benton. Copyright © 1943 by Alfred A. Knopf, Inc. and renewed 1971 by Walter Benton. Reprinted by permission of Alfred A. Knopf, a Division of Random House, Inc.

J. B. BERNSTEIN: "Bacchanalia," from *Alabaster Skull & Moonlit Roses* edited by J. B. Bernstein and Franz Douskey (New Haven, CT: Allegra Imagery and Printing, 2000). Copyright © 2000 by J. B. Bernstein. Reprinted by permission of the author.

ELIZABETH BARRETT BROWNING: "I flung closer to his breast...," from *Aurora Leigh* by Elizabeth Barrett Browning, edited by Margaret Reynolds (Athens, OH: Ohio University Press/Swallow Press, 1992). Reprinted by permission of Ohio University Press/Swallow Press, Athens, Ohio.

ELIZABETH CLAMAN: "Love and Desire," from *Passionate Lives* by Elizabeth Claman (Eugene, OR: Queen of Swords Press, 1998), p. 188. Copyright © 1998 by Elizabeth Claman. Reprinted by permission of Queen of Swords Press.

E. E. CUMMINGS: "O It's Nice To Get Up In,the slipshod mucous kiss," from *Complete Poems: 1904–1962* by E. E. Cummings, edited by George J. Firmage. Copyright 1923, 1925, 1951, 1953, © 1991 by the Trustees for the E. E. Cummings Trust. Copyright © 1976 by George J. Firmage. Reprinted by permission of Liveright Publishing Corporation.

LUCILLE LANG DAY: "Fire," from *Fire in the Garden* by Lucille Lang Day (Berkeley, CA: Mother's Hen, 1997), p. 25. Originally appeared in *Tunnel Road: A Poetry Anthology* (Orinda, CA: John F. Kennedy University Press, 1979), p. 14. Copyright © 1979 by Lucille Lang Day. Reprinted by permission of the poet.

EMILY DICKINSON: "Wild Nights—Wild Nights!" from *The Poems of Emily Dickinson*, edited by Ralph Franklin (Cambridge, MA: The Belknap Press of Harvard University Press). Copyright © 1998 by the President and Fellows of Harvard College. Copyright © 1951, 1955, 1979 by the President and Fellows of Harvard College. Reprinted by permission of the publishers and trustees of Amherst College.

STEPHEN DUNN: "The Night the Children Were Away," from *Local Time* by Stephen Dunn (William Morrow Co., 1986). Copyright © 1986 by Stephen Dunn. Reprinted by permission of the poet.

GAYLE ELEANOR: "Awakening" appeared in *The Dancing Rose Anthology* (New London, CT: Full Moon Press, 1999), vol. 4, p. 31. Copyright © 1999 by Gayle Eleanor. Reprinted by permission of the poet.

EMANI: "Public Affection" appeared in *Passionate Lives* (Eugene, OR: Queen

ABOUT THE EDITOR

Wendy Maltz, M.S.W., is a nationally recognized psychotherapist and lecturer on healthy sexuality and sexual healing. She is coauthor of *Private Thoughts: Exploring the Power of Women's Sexual Fantasies*, editor of *Passionate Hearts: The Poetry of Sexual Love*, author of *The Sexual Healing Journey: A Guide for Survivors of Sexual Abuse*, and coauthor of *Incest and Sexuality: A Guide to Understanding and Healing*. Wendy has written and narrated two video productions, "Partners in Healing" and "Relearning Touch," for couples healing the intimate repercussions of sexual abuse and addiction. She is codirector, with her husband Larry, of Maltz Counseling Associates in Eugene, Oregon. Her website is www.healthysex.com.